UBUNTU
HACKS™

Other Linux resources from O'Reilly

Related titles	Knoppix Hacks™ Linux Cookbook™ Linux Desktop Hacks™ Linux in a Nutshell Linux Multimedia Hacks™	Linux Network Administrator's Guide Linux Server Hacks™ Running Linux

Hacks Series Home *hacks.oreilly.com* is a community site for developers and power users of all stripes. Readers learn from each other as they share their favorite tips and tools for Mac OS X, Linux, Google, Windows XP, and more.

Linux Books Resource Center *linux.oreilly.com* is a complete catalog of O'Reilly's books on Linux and Unix and related technologies, including sample chapters and code examples.

ONLamp.com is the premier site for the open source web platform: Linux, Apache, MySQL and either Perl, Python, or PHP.

Conferences O'Reilly brings diverse innovators together to nurture the ideas that spark revolutionary industries. We specialize in documenting the latest tools and systems, translating the innovator's knowledge into useful skills for those in the trenches. Visit *conferences.oreilly.com* for our upcoming events.

Safari Bookshelf (*safari.oreilly.com*) is the premier online reference library for programmers and IT professionals. Conduct searches across more than 1,000 books. Subscribers can zero in on answers to time-critical questions in a matter of seconds. Read the books on your Bookshelf from cover to cover or simply flip to the page you need. Try it today for free.

UBUNTU HACKS™

*Jonathan Oxer, Kyle Rankin,
and Bill Childers*

O'REILLY®

Beijing · Cambridge · Farnham · Köln · Paris · Sebastopol · Taipei · Tokyo

Ubuntu Hacks™

by Jonathan Oxer, Kyle Rankin, and Bill Childers

Copyright © 2006 O'Reilly Media, Inc. All rights reserved.
Printed in the United States of America.

Published by O'Reilly Media, Inc., 1005 Gravenstein Highway North,
Sebastopol, CA 95472.

O'Reilly books may be purchased for educational, business, or sales promotional use. Online editions are also available for most titles (*safari.oreilly.com*). For more information, contact our corporate/institutional sales department: (800) 998-9938 or *corporate@oreilly.com*.

Editor: Brian Jepson
Production Editor: Sanders Kleinfeld
Copyeditor: Sanders Kleinfeld
Proofreader: Matt Hutchinson

Indexer: John Bickelhaupt
Cover Designer: Marcia Friedman
Interior Designer: David Futato
Illustrators: Robert Romano and Jessamyn Read

Printing History:

June 2006:   First Edition.

RepKover™ This book uses RepKover™, a durable and flexible lay-flat binding.

ISBN: 0-596-52720-9
[M]

Co

Credits

About the Authors

Jonathan Oxer (*http://jon.oxer.com.au/*) is president of Linux Australia, the national organization for Linux users and developers. He is the author of "How To Build A Website And Stay Sane" (*http://www.stay-sane.com*), writes regularly for *The Age* and *Sydney Morning Herald* newspapers, and his articles have been translated into French, Brazilian Portuguese, Italian, Norwegian, and Spanish and have appeared in dozens of publications.

In 1994, he founded one of the first businesses in the world to specialize in dynamic web sites and online content management, and in 1995 he became one of the first people to ever do real-time event coverage via the Internet when a live feed was run from the floor of the Bicycle Industry Trade Show in Sydney, Australia. His company, Internet Vision Technologies (*http://www.ivt.com.au*), has since developed web sites, intranets, extranets, and custom web applications for clients ranging from backyard businesses to multinational corporations.

Jonathan has been a Debian developer since 2002 and has convened the Debian Miniconf in a different city every year since 2003. He has presented dozens of tutorials, papers, and keynotes on various technology and business topics at both corporate and government seminars; at conferences, including LinuxTag, linux.conf.au, Open Source Developers Conference, and Debian Miniconf; and at user groups, including Melbourne PHP User Group and Linux Users Victoria. He sits on the Advisory Group of Swinburne University's Centre for Collaborative Business Innovation, which is responsible for researching and formulating IT-related, post-graduate curriculum strategies, and on the Australian Federal government's e-Research Coordinating Committee Reference Group.

He lives in Melbourne, Australia with his wife, daughter, and son.

Kyle Rankin is a system administrator for QuinStreet, Inc., the current president of the North Bay Linux Users Group, and the author of *Knoppix Hacks*, *Knoppix Pocket Reference*, and *Linux Multimedia Hacks* (all from O'Reilly). Kyle has been using Linux in one form or another since early 1998. In his free time, he either writes or does pretty much the same thing he does at work: works with Linux.

Bill Childers is Director of Enterprise Systems for Quinstreet, Inc. He's been working with Linux and Unix since before it was cool, and previously worked for Sun Microsystems and Set Engineering. In his spare time, he works with the Gilroy Garlic Festival Association as one of its chairmen, and enjoys playing with his children.

Contributors

- Scott Granneman specializes in helping schools, nonprofits, and businesses harness emerging technologies. Through presentations, consulting, and publications, Scott explicates the power of the Internet, the World Wide Web, and related technologies. He has helped educate thousands of people of all ages—from preteens to senior citizens—on a wide variety of topics. A mix of educational experience and practical knowhow enables Scott to deliver the kind of hands-on solutions his clients expect. And, as the Internet continues its phenomenal growth, he helps his clients take full advantage of each new evolution of this emerging technology. Detailed information is available at *www.granneman.com*.

- Brian Jepson is an O'Reilly editor, programmer, and coauthor of *Mac OS X Tiger for Unix Geeks* and *Learning Unix for Mac OS X Panther*. He's also a volunteer system administrator and all-around geek for AS220, a nonprofit arts center in Providence, Rhode Island. AS220 gives Rhode Island artists uncensored and unjuried forums for their work. These forums include galleries, performance space, and publications. Brian sees to it that technology, especially free software, supports that mission.

- Thomas Pletcher operates a communications agency in upstate New York using Ubuntu and other free and open source software. He is also a writer/partner at CommunityMX.com. He and his wife Barbara operate a site (*http://www.pfne.org/rescue*) devoted to rescuing Great Pyrenees dogs, a wonderful breed he hopes to see on the cover of an O'Reilly book before long.

Acknowledgments

The authors would like to thank the people who made this book possible.

Jonathan

The biggest thanks definitely have to go to my wife Ann and our children Amelia and Thomas, who for several months barely saw me from one week to the next. Writing *Ubuntu Hacks* has been one of those periods when everything else, including sleep, became secondary to just getting the job done, and my family was amazingly supportive and understanding through everything.

Thanks also to my coauthors Kyle Rankin and Bill Childers, who so willingly shared their knowledge of all things Linux, and the contributing writers who put in a big effort to supplement the body of the text with their particular areas of expertise. And the whole *Ubuntu Hacks* circus wouldn't have been possible without our editor, Brian Jepson, acting as ringmaster and keeping all our performances on schedule while even managing to contribute some of his own.

Finally, without the Canonical team there wouldn't be an Ubuntu to hack on, and without Debian there would never have been Canonical, and without the whole free/open source software community there would never have been Debian, so the ultimate thanks have to go to the amazing community that we're all part of. To every person who has ever written open source software, or submitted a bug report, or written a how-to, or maintained a Debian package, or stood on a street corner and handed out Ubuntu CDs: thank you. This book is written in your honor.

Kyle

First I'd like to thank my wife Joy for helping me yet again through the crunch period of this book. I'd also like to thank David Brickner for bringing me on this project, along with Brian Jepson for his guidance in editing the book.

This book was the result of a great team effort, so many thanks to Bill and Jon for all their hard work to make the book happen, and thanks to all the contributing writers.

Finally, I'd like to thank Ubuntu's amazing community of users and developers for their hard work in making Ubuntu a success in such a short amount of time.

Bill

I want to kick off this acknowledgments section by thanking and recognizing the most important people in my life: my family. Gillian and Conner, this book is for you. This is why Daddy's been at the keyboard for so many nights and weekends. Special thanks to Kelly for putting up with me while I undertook this project amongst all the other things I do—I love you, honey. You've been a tremendous influence and source of support, and I couldn't have pulled any of this off without you.

Thanks to my parents and grandparents for getting me my first computer and supporting my initial "addiction"—I wouldn't be where I am today without them.

Thanks to all the programmers, documentation people, bug testers, and everyone else who contributes to the Ubuntu and Debian projects. Every one of you should be proud of your work—you've created something truly special. Thanks to the crowd of *#linux* too, particularly Jorge, whose ongoing pursuit of shiny stuff led me to run the prerelease of Warty way back when. Also thanks to my fellow writer Kyle: all the stuff we've been through has been a total blast, and I'm looking forward to the future.

Finally, thanks to David Brickner and Brian Jepson for giving me this shot and for editing all my mistaeks (sic).

Preface

The first release of Ubuntu, the Warty Warthog, was made available to the world on October 20, 2004. Less than two years later, Ubuntu is now the number-one most popular Linux version at DistroWatch.com, far ahead of the distribution in second place. Countless articles, reviews, and blog postings have been written about Ubuntu and its sister distros, Kubuntu and Edubuntu. In Macedonia, Ubuntu will be installed in 468 schools and 182 computer labs. In South Africa, HP is going to offer desktops and notebooks with Ubuntu on them. Around the world, hundreds of thousands of people have installed Ubuntu, and, in many cases, it was the first Linux distro they'd ever tried. For many of those new Linux users, Ubuntu has been so good that they've switched to Linux. For a Linux distro that's still an infant, this is remarkable stuff!

Why has Ubuntu been so successful? Technically, it's based on Debian, which is an excellent foundation for a Linux distro, but Ubuntu has added a level of finish and polish that has made it a joy to use for newbies, though it is still a powerhouse for more experienced users. It's incredibly up-to-date; a team of dedicated developers ensures that everything "just works," with regular updates to the various packages that make up the distro and a roughly six-month release schedule between distros.

But the secret behind the phenomenal success and growth of Ubuntu is really one man: South African Mark Shuttleworth. After founding Thawte, a company providing digital certificates, when he was 22, Shuttleworth sold the company four years later to VeriSign for a large amount of money. After fulfilling his dream of going into space, he decided to fulfill another and build the best Linux distro in the world. In that he has succeeded.

But it's also about principles with Shuttleworth. He has plenty of money, and he wants to do things with his fortune that will change the world. Consequently, Ubuntu will always aim for the highest quality, and it will always

be free. The name *Ubuntu* itself is laden with meaning, as it is an African word meaning both "humanity to others" and "I am what I am because of who we all are," while *Kubuntu* means "towards humanity." Shuttleworth has promulgated the Ubuntu Code of Conduct, which states that members of the community must practice consideration, respect, and collaboration.

This is a book written by passionate Ubuntu and Kubuntu users who are excited to talk about a powerful, cool distro that meets the needs of novice, intermediate, and experienced users in a wide variety of ways. The hacks in this book cover the essential areas of Ubuntu, and they'll help you maximize your use of the distro. Whether you want to play music and movies, or use Ubuntu on your laptop as you travel, or install just about any software package you could ever want, or run other operating systems inside Ubuntu, we've got it all covered.

We know you'll get a lot out of *Ubuntu Hacks*, but we also want to encourage you to give back to the community and help grow Ubuntu:

- Visit the main Ubuntu and Kubuntu web sites at *http://www.ubuntu.com* and *http://www.kubuntu.org*. The entire sites are worth exploring in depth, but the Wikis especially offer a wealth of useful information.

- Download Ubuntu and offer it to friends, family, and acquaintances. Heck, offer it to total strangers! The more people who try Ubuntu, the more people who will use Ubuntu.

- If you don't want to download the distro, you can request free CDs at *https://shipit.ubuntu.com*. Don't be shy—ask and ye shall receive!

- If you know how to program, consider becoming a Ubuntu developer. If you don't know how to program, there's still plenty of work you can do. Either way, head over to *http://www.ubuntu.com/developers*. If you think you have the right stuff, you can even apply for work at *http://www. ubuntu.com/employment*.

- Buy some Ubuntu swag from the Ubuntu Shop (*http://www.cafepress.com/ ubuntushop/*), or donate money at *http://www.ubuntu.com/donations*.

Most importantly, tell the world about Ubuntu! Let's get the word out: there's an awesome, free, super-powerful operating system that anyone can use named Ubuntu, and it's made for you.

Why Ubuntu Hacks?

The term *hacking* has a bad reputation in the press. They use it to refer to people who break into systems or wreak havoc with computers as their weapon. Among people who write code, though, the term *hack* refers to a "quick-and-dirty" solution to a problem, or a clever way to get something

done. And the term *hacker* is taken very much as a compliment, referring to someone as being *creative*, having the technical chops to get things done. The Hacks series is an attempt to reclaim the word, document the good ways people are hacking, and pass the hacker ethic of creative participation on to the uninitiated. Seeing how others approach systems and problems is often the quickest way to learn about a new technology.

How to Use This Book

You can read this book from cover to cover if you like, but each hack stands on its own, so feel free to browse and jump to the different sections that interest you most. If there's a prerequisite you need to know about, a cross-reference will guide you to the right hack.

How This Book Is Organized

This book is divided into 10 chapters, organized by subject:

Chapter 1, *Getting Started*

This chapter shows you how to get started with Ubuntu. Whether you want to give it a whirl with a live CD, or you're ready to jump right in and install Ubuntu on your computer, you'll find what you need here. In addition to getting all the information you need to install Ubuntu on your system, you'll also learn how to get started with the Linux command line, set up your printer, file a bug report, and more.

Chapter 2, *The Linux Desktop*

You're going to spend a lot of time in front of a mouse, keyboard, and monitor, working with one of the Linux desktops. This chapter helps you get the most out of the GNOME and KDE desktop environments for Linux, and even helps you find out about a few others that are worth checking out. You'll also learn such things as how to get Java set up, how to work with files on remote computers, and how to get Ubuntu talking to handheld computers.

Chapter 3, *Multimedia*

This chapter gets the music and movies running so you can have some fun in between all the work you get done with Ubuntu. You'll learn how to play nearly any kind of audio and video, and burn files, music, and movies to optical discs.

Chapter 4, *Mobile Ubuntu*

If you're using Ubuntu on a notebook computer, you're probably going to want to cut a few wires. This chapter helps you get going with various wireless cards. You'll also learn how to get the most out of your laptop, from saving energy to installing add-on cards.

Chapter 5, *X11*

This chapter shows you how to tweak X11, the windowing system that lurks beneath the shiny veneer of KDE and GNOME. You'll learn how to get your mouse and keyboard working just right, and also how to get X11 configured so it takes full advantage of the graphics adapter in your computer.

Chapter 6, *Package Management*

To some extent, any Linux distribution is a big collection of packages held together by a whole lot of interesting and useful glue. Ubuntu's great advantage is the quality of those packings and all the testing and improvement that goes into them. This chapter shows you how to work with packages, whether you're installing them, finding new ones from beyond the edges of the Ubuntu universe, or creating your own.

Chapter 7, *Security*

This chapter shows you how to tighten up security on your system. You'll learn the basics of how the *sudo* command keeps you and your fellow users out of trouble, how to protect your network from intruders, and even how to keep your data safe if one of the bad guys does make it in.

Chapter 8, *Administration*

Every now and then, you're going to have to take a break from the fun of using Ubuntu and do some administrative tasks. Whether you're adding a new user, tweaking your system's configuration, or doing those backups you should have done long ago, you'll find what you need in this chapter.

Chapter 9, *Virtualization and Emulation*

This chapter shows you how to run Ubuntu inside of other operating systems, and other operating systems inside of Ubuntu. It's all made possible by a combination of emulation and virtualization, which effectively lets you run a computer inside of a computer.

Chapter 10, *Small Office/Home Office Server*

Ubuntu isn't just a great desktop operating system; it also makes a fantastic basis for a server. In this chapter, you'll learn everything from doing a basic server install to installing network services such as DNS, mail, Apache, and more.

Conventions Used in This Book

The following is a list of the typographical conventions used in this book:

Italic

> Used for emphasis and new terms where they are defined, as well as to indicate Unix utilities, URLs, filenames, filename extensions, and directory/folder names. For example, a path in the filesystem will appear as */usr/local*.

`Constant width`

> Used to show code examples, the contents of files, and console output, as well as the names of variables, commands, and other code excerpts.

`Constant width bold`

> Used to highlight portions of code, either for emphasis or to indicate text that should be typed by the user.

`Constant width italic`

> Used in code examples to show sample text to be replaced with your own values.

Gray type

> Used to indicate a cross-reference within the text.

↵

> Used in file contents at the end of a line of code to indicate that it carries over to the following line because of space limitations. You should enter these lines as one line in the actual files.

You should pay special attention to notes set apart from the text with the following icons:

> This is a tip, suggestion, or general note. It contains useful supplementary information about the topic at hand.

> This is a warning or note of caution, often indicating that your money or your privacy might be at risk.

The thermometer icons, found next to each hack, indicate the relative complexity of the hack:

beginner   moderate   expert

Using Code Examples

This book is here to help you get your job done. In general, you may use the code in this book in your programs and documentation. You do not need to contact us for permission unless you're reproducing a significant portion of the code. For example, writing a program that uses several chunks of code from this book does not require permission. Selling or distributing a CD-ROM of examples from O'Reilly books *does* require permission. Answering a question by citing this book and quoting example code does not require permission. Incorporating a significant amount of example code from this book into your product's documentation does require permission.

We appreciate, but do not require, attribution. An attribution usually includes the title, author, publisher, and ISBN. For example: "*Ubuntu Hacks* by Jonathan Oxer, Kyle Rankin, and Bill Childers. Copyright 2006 O'Reilly Media, Inc., 0-596-52720-9."

If you feel your use of code examples falls outside fair use or the permission given above, feel free to contact us at *permissions@oreilly.com*.

Safari® Enabled

 When you see a Safari® Enabled icon on the cover of your favorite technology book, that means the book is available online through the O'Reilly Network Safari Bookshelf.

Safari offers a solution that's better than e-books. It's a virtual library that lets you easily search thousands of top tech books, cut and paste code samples, download chapters, and find quick answers when you need the most accurate, current information. Try it for free at *http://safari.oreilly.com*.

How to Contact Us

We have tested and verified the information in this book to the best of our ability, but you may find that features have changed (or even that we have made mistakes!). As a reader of this book, you can help us to improve future editions by sending us your feedback. Please let us know about any errors, inaccuracies, bugs, misleading or confusing statements, and typos that you find anywhere in this book.

Please also let us know what we can do to make this book more useful to you. We take your comments seriously and will try to incorporate reasonable suggestions into future editions. You can write to us at:

O'Reilly Media, Inc.
1005 Gravenstein Highway North
Sebastopol, CA 95472
800-998-9938 (in the U.S. or Canada)
707-829-0515 (international/local)
707-829-0104 (fax)

To ask technical questions or to comment on the book, send email to:

bookquestions@oreilly.com

The web site for *Ubuntu Hacks* lists examples, errata, and plans for future editions. You can find this page at:

http://www.oreilly.com/catalog/ubuntuhks/

For more information about this book and others, see the O'Reilly web site:

http://www.oreilly.com

Got a Hack?

To explore Hacks books online or to contribute a hack for future titles, visit:

http://hacks.oreilly.com

Getting Started

Hacks 1–14

An operating system takes some getting used to. Whether you are new to Ubuntu or new to Linux itself, there are some basic things you need to get familiar with before you can move on. The hacks in this chapter cover those basics and then some.

The Ubuntu Live CD is a good way to explore Ubuntu without changing anything on your hard drive. This chapter explains how to get up and running with the Live CD, and even shows you how to use it with a memory stick to keep your settings and documents around between reboots. You'll also learn how to install Ubuntu, whether you want to make it the sole operating system on your computer or want to dual-boot between Ubuntu and Windows. You'll even learn how to install Ubuntu on a Macintosh.

This chapter also covers fundamentals such as getting your printer set up, getting help (and helping Ubuntu by submitting bug reports), getting started with the command line, and finding the most important applications you need to start "doing stuff" with Ubuntu.

Test-Drive Ubuntu

HACK #1

Use the Ubuntu Live CD to get to know Linux before installing it on your system. This is simply the fastest and safest way to try out Linux.

Though Linux on the desktop looks and behaves a lot like Windows, the simple fact is it isn't. Your favorite Windows programs probably won't run in Linux, it may be difficult to migrate data from your Windows install [Hack #7], and the years you've spent getting used to how Windows does things will prove mostly useless when it comes to understanding how Linux works. With all of this in mind, wouldn't it be great if you could try out Linux without spending hours or days getting it installed and configured on your system? Well, you can. With the Ubuntu Live CD, you can take Linux for a test-drive to be certain you really want to commit the time and resources to

running it full-time. This hack shows you how to download the Ubuntu Live CD and boot your system using it. Other hacks in the book show you how to get around in GNOME **[Hack #15]** or KDE **[Hack #16]**, the two popular graphical environments that run on top of Linux.

Downloading the Live CD

A *live CD* is a complete installation of Linux that runs entirely from CD. While you are using a live CD, nothing is written to your hard drive, so your Windows or Mac OS installation is not affected in any way. However, because you're running from a CD, you're limited to using only the programs that are installed on the CD, and everything will run a bit slower because CD access is much slower than that of a hard drive. Still, even with these limitations, it's undeniable that a live CD is the easiest way to try out Ubuntu.

You can obtain the Ubuntu Live CD from the main Ubuntu web site (*http://www.ubuntulinux.org*). There is a convenient Download link that takes you right to the download page to get the latest released version of Ubuntu. This hack, indeed this entire book, was written for the Dapper Drake release—version 6.06, LTS—because it is the release that will be supported for the next five years (previous Ubuntu releases were supported for only 12 months). Ubuntu versions are numbered according to the year and month of release; therefore, this version of Dapper Drake was released in June 2006. Regardless of which version you download, the hacks in this book should be valid for a long time to come.

> LTS stands for Long Term Support, which indicates that this release of Ubuntu is supported for three years on the desktop, and five years on the server.

The file you want to download is the ISO image that corresponds to the computer type you are using. If you're on a PC, this probably means the x86 version, but if you happen to be using a 64-bit AMD or Intel processor, you want to download the 64-bit PC version. Finally, if you're a Mac user, you want to get the PowerPC version. It is unknown at the time of this writing if Ubuntu will support the new Macintoshes with Intel processors.

You can burn the ISO image to disc using any CD-burning software you have installed on your computer. Make sure you choose the option that burns the image to disc; don't select the option to burn a data CD that will just copy the image over as a file. The difference is that the former will create a bootable disc, and the latter will not.

Booting the CD

To use a live CD, you typically need do nothing more than boot your computer with the CD already in the optical drive. Most Windows computers these days are preconfigured to boot from a CD or DVD before booting from the hard drive. We fancy this is because users often need to restore or repair their Windows installation using the OEM-provided restore CD, and this configuration saves a lot of calls to technical support.

> If you are using a Mac, you need to hold down the C key to boot from a CD.

But, if for some reason your Windows computer doesn't want to boot from the CD, the fix is usually quite simple. You need to boot into your computer's BIOS and modify the setting that specifies the boot order. Getting into the BIOS usually requires you to press a key early on in the boot sequence. The key you press depends on the make of your computer and BIOS, but it is typically displayed on the splash screen that comes up when your computer starts (the one that announces the manufacturer of the computer, not the Windows splash screen). If your splash screen doesn't tell you this information, try one of these keys: Esc, Del, F2, F10, or F12.

> On some computers, F12 launches you directly into a boot selection menu, offering options such as booting from hard disk, floppy drive, USB drive, optical drive, or the network. This lets you boot from a different device without making changes to your BIOS configuration.

Once you're in the BIOS, you should look for a menu called Boot or one labeled Advanced Configuration. Under this menu, you should see a setting that allows you to specify that the CD or optical drive boot before the hard disk. There are hundreds of BIOS variants, so we can't be more specific than that, but if you look at every option screen, you will eventually see the setting you need to change as well as instructions for how to do so. Once you've made the change, save it, and then reboot your computer.

Hopefully, this will be the only problem you have booting from the Live CD. If you've configured the BIOS correctly, shortly after boot you should see a splash screen with the following options:

Run preinstalled live system
> This option loads the Live CD environment so you can test-drive Ubuntu. If you don't press any keys within 30 seconds of getting to this screen, this option will automatically execute.

Rescue a broken system

Choose this option to load a minimal Linux enviroment that you can use to troubleshoot a nonworking Linux installation.

Memory test

You can use this option to run a test of your computer's RAM. Many people don't realize it, but many odd computer problems can be traced to bad RAM modules. If your computer exhibits erratic behavior, such as frequent freezes or an inability to consistently finish booting, your RAM may be the culprit, and running this program may save you hours of frustration.

Boot from the first hard disk

Select this option to continue booting from the hard drive.

Unless you're troubleshooting, about the only other option of interest right now is pressing F2 to select a language. This setting determines the language and keyboard layout that will be used for the rest of the test-drive; the default is English.

Once you've made any necessary language selections, you should use the arrow keys to select "Run preinstalled live system," and press Enter. This begins the loading of Ubuntu. You'll see a lot of messages flash by on the screen and eventually be faced with a text dialog to configure your screen resolution. You can use the Tab and arrow keys to move the selection cursor, the spacebar to toggle a selection, and Enter to accept your input and move on to the next screen. You can select multiple entries, depending on what your monitor supports. Ubuntu will use the highest selected and supported resolution as the default.

After this, Ubuntu continues to load, and, if all goes well, you'll automatically be logged in to a GNOME desktop less than a minute later. Depending on your hardware (network, sound, printer, etc.), you may find everything preconfigured and working. If you don't, some of the hardware-configuration hacks later in this book may be useful even in the Live CD environment.

Another Use for the Live CD

The Ubuntu Live CD also includes Windows versions of several open source programs. To access these program installers from within Windows, just insert the live CD while logged in. Within a few seconds, the autoload feature of Windows should display a window that lets you launch each installer. If this doesn't happen, you can just open Windows Explorer, navigate to the CD, and use the installers found in the program directory. The programs on the CD are:

OpenOffice.org 2.0
> This is a free office suite that includes a word processor, spreadsheet, database, drawing program, and web page creator. OpenOffice.org (the *.org* is really a part of its name, but you can abbreviate it to OOo) can open and save to Microsoft Office formats, which means you may be able to use it in place of that office suite, or at the very least collaborate with others who do. You can learn more about OOo at the OpenOffice.org web site (*http://www.openoffice.org*).

Mozilla Firefox 1.5
> Firefox is a web-browsing alternative to Microsoft's Internet Explorer. This secure and feature-rich web browser took the computer world by storm in 2005 and became the first browser to gain market share against IE since the mid-90s. To learn more about Firefox, visit the Mozilla web site (*http://www.mozilla.org*). Pay particular attention to the information about tabs and extensions, two features that can dramatically enhance your browsing experience.

Gaim 1.5.0
> Gaim is a multiprotocol instant-messenger program. This means it can connect to multiple networks, such as AOL, MSN, Jabber, and Yahoo! all at the same time, making it easy for you to stay connected to your friends without having to run a separate chat client for each network.

Each of these programs is also part of the Ubuntu Live CD experience, so you can try them out before installing them to Windows. If you like the Live CD so much that you want to keep using it, be sure to check out "Make Live CD Data Persistent" **[Hack #3]**.

H A C K   Get Help
#2
Find out where to get more help on using Ubuntu. Forums, Wikis, IRC chat rooms, and a built-in help system stand at the ready.

Everybody needs a place to turn to when he gets stuck. One of the nice things about Ubuntu Linux is the amount of help you can receive, if you know where to look. The development team at Canonical has put together an excellent support infrastructure that includes both free and nonfree support solutions.

Web-Based Documentation

Your first stop on the support train should be the Ubuntu Support page at *http://www.ubuntulinux.org/support*. This page contains links for all the currently possible support methods, both official and unofficial, paid-for and free.

Of course, Ubuntu has excellent documentation. The official documentation effort at *http://help.ubuntu.com* has both a Quick Tour section and a comprehensive Start Guide. The Quick Tour page is a great flyer that advertises the high points of Ubuntu and shows off some screenshots, while the Start Guide is more of an overall how-to document.

The next place to visit if you're stuck should be the Ubuntu Wiki (*https://wiki.ubuntu.com*). The Wiki is extremely comprehensive and is constantly updated by Ubuntu users and developers. As a result, it's typically more up-to-date than the official documentation. One of the side benefits to the Ubuntu Wiki is the Laptop Testing area at *https://wiki.ubuntu.com/LaptopTestingTeam*. If you're about to install Ubuntu on a laptop, you might want to see if your model is on that page, since the Laptop Testing Team puts all its installation notes and tweaks on that area of the Wiki. It might save you a lot of work and could very well help you get a troublesome feature like wireless or power management working correctly under Ubuntu Linux.

Interactive Help and Support

If you have a question that you can't find the answer to, you can ask it in either the Ubuntu Forums or the Ubuntu IRC chat room. The Ubuntu Forums at *http://www.ubuntuforums.org* provide a nearly real-time support venue that you can also search. Odds are, if you're having a problem, someone else has already had that problem and asked for help on the forums. If you have a more urgent issue, or just want instant gratification, you can ask for help in the IRC chat room. The IRC room is located on the *freenode* network (*irc.freenode.net*), and it's called *#ubuntu*. If you've never used IRC before, just click on the Applications menu, select Internet, and launch Xchat. (If you don't see Xchat on the menu, go to System → Administration → Synaptic Package Manager [Hack #55] and install *xchat-gnome*.) Log in to *irc.freenode.net* and join the *#ubuntu* channel. Once you're online, ask your question, but be sure to provide as much detail as possible for the people in the room. Please note that most of the people there are volunteers who are contributing to the Ubuntu effort by trying to offer support, so be friendly and be prepared to answer questions that anyone in the room may ask in return, since they may need more information to figure out your issue. You might want to lurk in the channel for a while and read the messages that scroll by to get a feel for the tone and flow before you ask your question.

A lot of the work that makes Ubuntu what it is happens on mailing lists. There's a comprehensive list of mailing lists at *https://lists.ubuntu.com/mailman/listinfo*; you can either search the archives of these lists, or you can add yourself to them and post your question there. If you choose to post a

question to one of these lists, please show proper etiquette and ensure your question is targeted at the correct mailing list. As with IRC, it's worth spending some time to get familiar with the mailing lists: read some older posts and responses, and pay attention to which questions get answers and which ones don't.

Traditional Pay-per-Incident Support

If you can't get a solution to your problem through the aforementioned free methods, there's always paid-for support through Canonical and other organizations. The page at *http://www.ubuntu.com/support/supportoptions/paidsupport* details the various options open to you for paid support. If you're considering using Ubuntu in a corporate environment, you should become familiar with this page.

> If you purchase paid-for support from Canonical, you'll get a service-level agreement that guarantees you a response within a reasonable time frame, as well as direct access to the core Ubuntu developers, which is something that the free support does not offer.

Whatever your need, the Canonical team and the larger Ubuntu community should have it covered. The support community is widespread, knowledgeable, and ready to help, so don't let a snag in your installation damage your Ubuntu experience!

HACK #3 Make Live CD Data Persistent

Take your desktop with you on a USB stick and access it anywhere with the Ubuntu Live CD.

Wouldn't it be handy if you could walk up to any random computer, insert a copy of the Ubuntu Live CD, plug in a USB key, boot it up, and have a fully working system with your own documents, settings, and programs—without modifying the computer in any way?

A little-known feature of the Ubuntu Dapper Drake Live CD allows you to do exactly that. When it starts up, it searches for a volume that has been given the label *casper-cow* and uses it to store documents, themes, and even extra programs that you install. This is far more powerful than just booting up a live CD and mounting a memory stick as your home directory because it's not restricted to just storing your documents. It gives you the flexibility of a fully installed system, while retaining the "go anywhere" feature of a live CD.

You can perform this trick with just about any storage device, including removable USB hard disks and compact flash drives, but for this hack we use a USB memory stick because they're cheap, portable, and commonly available in increasingly large capacities.

Set the Label on Your USB Memory Stick

Connect the USB memory stick to a computer running Ubuntu. Ubuntu will probably mount it automatically, so the first thing to do is to find the device name that it has been assigned. Open Applications → Accessories → Terminal and type the following at the shell prompt:

```
$ df -h
```

to see a list of mounted volumes. The output should look something like this:

```
Filesystem        Size  Used Avail Use% Mounted on
/dev/hda3          54G   19G   35G  36% /
varrun            506M   84K  506M   1% /var/run
varlock           506M     0  506M   0% /var/lock
udev              506M  116K  506M   1% /dev
devshm            506M     0  506M   0% /dev/shm
/dev/hda1         221M   28M  181M  14% /boot
/dev/sda1         498M  214M  285M  43% /media/usbdisk
```

USB storage devices are emulated as SCSI devices by Linux, and you can see the last device is listed as */dev/sda1*. This means SCSI device A, partition 1. If you have anything on the memory stick that you want to save, now is the time to copy it onto your computer, because you're about to totally erase it.

Once you've backed up your files, it's time to unmount the device:

```
$ sudo umount /dev/sda1
```

Ubuntu is smart enough to figure out if you are "in" the device (either on the command line or using the file browser), so if the system refuses to unmount because the device is still in use, just close any other windows you have open and try again.

Then create a new filesystem with the correct label:

```
$ sudo mkfs.ext3 -b 4096 -L casper-cow /dev/sda1
```

You must replace */dev/sda1* with the actual device name used by your memory stick. If you have other USB devices attached, it is possible that one of them has claimed this device name. If in doubt, run the command *dmesg* right after you plug in the memory stick. You should see a message indicating the name of the device that was used to represent your memory stick.

This will create an *ext3* journaling filesystem, which is a good choice for general-purpose use, but, if you prefer, you can use any filesystem that's supported by the Live CD. The *mkfs.ext3* command will report some statistics about the new filesystem, and then you're ready to try it out.

Boot the Live CD in Persistent Mode

Plug your USB memory stick into the target machine, power up the computer, and quickly insert the Dapper Drake Live CD. If the computer is not configured to boot from CD-ROM, you may need to press a key (typically Del or F2) at startup to enter the BIOS settings menu; you then need to change the order of the boot devices to put CD-ROM at the top of the list, and then select the Exit option (the one that saves your changes to the BIOS) from the BIOS menu. The computer will then boot up again and look for the Live CD before attempting to boot from the hard disk. Some computers have a menu (often activated by F12) that lets you choose which device to boot from without having to make changes to your BIOS.

> If you are using a Mac, you need to hold down the C key to boot from a CD.

When the Live CD starts up, you will see a menu. Normally, you would just press Enter to start the boot process, but instead, press F4 to access the Other Options menu that allows you to start up the Live CD in special modes. You'll see a list of the arguments that will be passed to the kernel on startup; just add a space and type persistent, then hit Enter.

That's it!

Testing Persistence

The computer will now boot from the Live CD in persistent mode, but you won't see anything different. In fact, it can be quite hard to tell if it even worked or not. As a simple test, you can try changing something obvious, such as your desktop picture, and then you can log out and reboot the computer back into persistent mode. If everything worked properly, your desktop picture will still be set as you specified.

Try changing other things on your system such as creating documents or even installing extra software. Changes you make should be preserved even after you reboot the system.

How It Works

The Live CD is a read-only environment, so of course you can't save changes made to the running system straight to the CD. However, when running in persistent mode, the system on the Live CD allows items on your memory stick to override items within the Live CD environment. In the test described in this hack, you changed the desktop image; this caused Ubuntu to save your new desktop picture and settings onto the *casper-cow* device. The next time the Live CD sets the desktop, it detects that a new setting has been stored on the device and applies it instead of the default setting. The Live CD therefore provides the basic data for a complete, functional environment, and any changes you make to that environment are written to the removable device and used to override the default settings.

HACK #4   Customize the Ubuntu Live CD

Rip, burn, and boot to create a personalized version of the Ubuntu Live CD with your choice of software and documents.

The Ubuntu Live CD [Hack #1] contains a complete Ubuntu installation that can run directly from the CD itself, without needing to be installed onto a hard disk. It's ideal for demonstrating Linux on computers with another operating system installed because after you take the CD out and reboot the computer, it returns to the exact state it was in originally. It's a totally painless way to take Linux for a test run with no risk.

The Live CD is also extremely useful for recovering an unbootable machine: just pop in the Live CD and reboot, and you will have a fully running Linux system from which you can access the internal hard disk, copy files across the network, or do whatever else you need to do to fix the system. And you can even use a memory stick [Hack #3] to store changes made inside the Live CD environment.

The Ubuntu Live CD starts up a full desktop environment that's functionally identical to a standard Ubuntu installation, but perhaps you want a Live CD that contains specific software or documents to suit your environment. For example, you may want to create a Live CD that boots up a machine as a fully configured router and firewall with no hard disk. Or maybe you want a forensics disk preloaded with virus-scanning and network-analysis tools plus the checksums of important files.

No problem. You can create a customized version of the Ubuntu Live CD configured exactly the way you want it.

Basic Requirements

Building the disk image for the Live CD takes a huge amount of storage, so you'll need up to 5 GB of swap plus at least another 3 GB of disk space for storing the image. You'll also need tools for creating and mounting disk images.

Add extra swap. While the disk image is being compressed, *two copies* of it are held entirely in memory, so without a huge amount of swap, you won't be able to do the compression necessary to generate the ISO.

Don't worry if you don't already have a 5 GB swap partition. You can set up a temporary swapfile inside one of your existing partitions without having to reformat. Assuming you have at least 5 GB of free space inside */tmp* (usually in your root partition), you can create the extra swapfile with *dd*:

```
$ sudo dd if=/dev/zero of=/tmp/swap bs=1M count=5000
```

It can take a very long time to create the swapfile, so you'll need to be patient. Once the file itself has been created, you can set up a swap filesystem on it and activate your new swap:

```
$ sudo mkswap /tmp/swap
$ sudo swapon /tmp/swap
```

You don't need to disable your existing swap first. Linux is smart enough to handle multiple swap partitions simultaneously, so your system should now have a total swap space comprising the new 5 GB swapfile plus your existing swap.

Install the tools. To mount a disk image as a loopback device and generate the ISO for your custom Live CD, you will need the *cloop-utils* and *mkisofs* packages, and to work with the *squashfs* compressed image on the Live CD, you'll need the *squashfs-tools* package:

```
$ sudo apt-get install cloop-utils mkisofs squashfs-tools
```

Standard Live CD. While it's possible to build a Live CD from scratch, it's much easier to start by modifying the standard Ubuntu Live CD. You can download the Live CD ISO disk image from *http://cdimage.ubuntu.com/* or use one of the CDs available from Canonical through the ShipIt program (*https://shipit.ubuntu.com/*).

Prepare Original Image

Make sure your locale is set to C to prevent Unicode problems with the build process:

```
$ export LC_ALL=C
```

Mount the original Ubuntu Live CD ISO image as a loopback device:

```
$ mkdir ~/mnt
$ sudo mount dapper-live-i386.iso ~/mnt -o loop
```

This will mount the CD image inside your home directory at ~/mnt. You can use an alternative location or mount the actual Live CD in your CD-ROM drive if you prefer.

Copy everything from the mounted image into a working directory, but make sure you skip the *filesystem.squashfs* compressed filesystem because you'll need to extract that separately. You can use *rsync* to make it easy:

```
$ rsync --exclude=/casper/filesystem.squashfs -a ~/mnt/ ~/extracted_cd
```

Next, extract the compressed filesystem. The Dapper Live CD uses the *squashfs* read-only filesystem, unlike previous Ubuntu Live CDs, which just used *cloop* filesystems. To work with *squashfs*, you will need to load the *squashfs* kernel module:

```
$ sudo modprobe squashfs
```

Now you can mount it and copy it onto your local hard disk:

```
$ mkdir squash
$ sudo mount -o loop ~/mnt/casper/filesystem.squashfs squash
$ sudo cp -a squash extracted_fs
```

Be prepared to wait quite a while for this to run. Once it's finished, you will have a complete, extracted copy of the Live CD image, so you can unmount the original:

```
$ sudo umount ~/mnt
```

Set Up the Target Filesystem

Mount the *proc* and *sys* virtual filesystems into your target:

```
$ sudo mount -t proc proc ~/extracted_fs/proc
$ sudo mount -t sysfs sysfs ~/extracted_fs/sys
```

In a moment, you'll be chrooting into the CD image, so if there are files you will need on your customized CD, the easiest thing to do is mount */home* into it:

```
$ sudo mount -o bind /home ~/extracted_fs/home
```

Then, once you are in the chroot, you will have full access to any files stored in your home directory.

Apply Customizations

Use *chroot* to enter the filesystem image:

```
$ sudo chroot ~/extracted_fs/ /bin/sh
```

Now, as far as you're concerned, you're running on a read/write installation of the Live CD. From there, you can use the usual package tools to update programs installed on the Live CD.

Delete unnecessary packages. The default Live CD is fairly full, so if you want to install extra packages, you will probably need to make some room first. If you want some ideas about which packages to remove, you can create a list of installed packages sorted by size using this command:

```
$ dpkg-query -W --showformat='${Installed-Size;10} ${Package}\n' | \
    sort -gr | less
```

Be very careful, though, because some packages are essential for the system to work at all. The GNOME Live CD is based on Ubuntu, so if you're looking for inspiration for which packages you can safely remove, you can start by looking at its configuration file, available at *http://cvs.gnome.org/viewcvs/livecd-project/livecd.conf?view=markup*.

Once you've settled on some packages to remove, you can uninstall them using *dpkg*:

```
$ sudo dpkg -r --purge packagename
```

Install additional packages. The regular network-based package tools won't work inside the chroot, so unfortunately it's not as simple as apt-get install *foo* to add packages. There are a number of ways around it, such as copying in a *hosts* file with the addresses of repository servers pre-resolved, because you can't do DNS lookups inside the chroot.

The simplest way, though, is probably just to predownload some packages into your home directory and use *dpkg* to install them after entering the chroot.

One very cool trick to simplify this process is to run the Synaptic package manager on your host system, find and mark the packages you want to install on your Live CD, and then select File → "Generate package download script." You will then have a script that you can execute to fetch and save the packages locally, storing them in your home directory for access from the chroot.

Customize the home directory. When the Live CD boots, it creates the user's home directory from scratch each time, using the files in */etc/skel*. If you have specific files you want to include in the home directory, you can put them in *skel*.

Unmount Customized Image

Now that all your changes have been applied, exit the chroot and then unmount the various filesystems:

```
$ exit
$ sudo umount ~/extracted_fs/home
$ sudo umount ~/extracted_fs/sys
$ sudo umount ~/extracted_fs/proc
```

Your customized filesystem is now ready to recompress, but first you need to generate a new manifest file that reflects the changes you have made to the list of installed packages. If you didn't actually install or remove any software, you can skip this step.

You can't perform this step using *sudo* (you have to really be running as *root*), so get a *root* shell with sudo -s:

```
$ sudo -s
```

Now generate the new manifest:

```
# chroot extracted_fs dpkg-query -W \
  --showformat='${Package} ${Version}\n' \
  > extracted_cd/casper/filesystem.manifest
```

You can exit the *root* shell now.

Repack the Filesystem

The new *squashfs* filesystem that will go inside the CD needs to be created:

```
$ sudo mksquashfs extracted_fs extracted_cd/casper/filesystem.squash
```

Once again, this stage can take a really long time.

The Live CD also needs to contain a checksum file that can be used to verify the integrity of the compressed filesystem. The checksum needs to be calculated from inside the CD image:

```
$ cd ~/extracted_cd
$ find . -type f -print0 | xargs -0 md5sum > md5sum.txt
```

Build the ISO

Everything up to this point has been architecture-independent, but the final stage of building the ISO itself depends on what type of system you are running:

x86 (i386) and x86_64 (amd64)
> Use the following command:
> ```
> $ sudo mkisofs -r -V "Custom Ubuntu 6.04 Live CD" \
>   -cache-inodes \
> ```

```
-J -l -b isolinux/isolinux.bin \
-c isolinux/boot.cat -no-emul-boot \
-boot-load-size 4 -boot-info-table \
-o custom-dapper-live-i386.iso extracted_cd
```

PowerPC

For PowerPC, it's necessary to download *hfs.map*:

```
$ wget http://people.ubuntu.com/~cjwatson/hfs.map
```

Then build the actual ISO:

```
$ sudo mkisofs -o new_image.iso -chrp-boot \
-U -part -hfs -T -r -l -J -A "application_id" \
-sysid PPC -V "volid" -volset 4 -volset-size 1 \
-volset-seqno 1 -hfs-volid "volume_name_hfs" \
-hfs-bless extracted_cd/install \
-map hfs.map -no-desktop -allow-multidot extracted_ppc_cd
```

IA64

Use the following command:

```
$ sudo mkisofs -r -V "Custom Ubuntu 6.04 Live CD ia64" \
-o custom-dapper-live-ia64.iso -no-emul-boot \
-J -b boot/boot.img -c boot/boot.catalog extracted_cd
```

Burn and Boot

You now have an ISO image of your customized Live CD, so burn it to a disc [Hack #33] and give it a try.

More Information and Scripts

The process of creating a customized Live CD is quite manual and laborious, but some of the steps above can be simplified using the *live_cd_tools* scripts that you can find online at *http://wiki.ubuntu.com/LiveCDCustomizationHowTo*. Note, however, that the process for building the Dapper Live CD is a bit different from the older process used by previous releases, such as Breezy, that used a compressed *loopback* filesystem instead of *squashfs*, so make sure you don't use scripts intended for the older process.

H A C K   Install Ubuntu

#5   Learn how to install Ubuntu on your computer.

If you've given Ubuntu a test-drive [Hack #1], or you're simply ready to dive into it sight unseen, all you need is an installation CD and a computer to install it on, and you can be up and running right away. There are a number of ways you can get an installation CD; if you've got broadband and a CD-R drive, you can probably get your hands on it in under an hour.

System Requirements

Ubuntu will run on just about any current personal computer. If you're using an Intel-compatible PC, it will probably "just work," since the kernel image that Ubuntu uses by default is optimized for the 80386, which means it will also be compatible with systems based on the 486, Pentium, and Pentium Pro, as well as the Pentium II, III, 4, and beyond, including all the other mainstream Intel-compatible CPUs such as the AMD Athlon and Sempron, as well as the Transmeta Crusoe and Efficeon. If your computer can run Windows 95 or later, it can probably run Ubuntu just fine. If you're running an AMD64 system, there is even a special version of Ubuntu you can download.

If you have a G3, G4, or G5 Macintosh, you'll probably be able to run the PowerPC version of Ubuntu. If it can run Mac OS X, it should be able to run Ubuntu. Mac users should see "Install Ubuntu on a Mac" [Hack #8] for complete details.

Although you may have a CPU that's compatible with Ubuntu, you may run into some hardware that doesn't want to play along. Wireless network cards can be particularly tricky, but after you get Ubuntu up and running, there are some tricks [Hacks #41 and #42] you can use to get them working. However, because the Ubuntu installer tries to use the network, I strongly urge you to keep an Ethernet cable handy in case you need to plug your system into a wired network for the install. (Early on, the Ubuntu installer will report which network interfaces it was able to activate, so if you don't see your wireless network adapter listed, it's time to use that Ethernet cable.)

Disk space and memory are probably your most important considerations. If you are planning on running the GNOME (Ubuntu) [Hack #15] or KDE (Kubuntu) [Hack #16] desktop environment, your computer will benefit from plenty of RAM and disk space. Consider 2 GB of disk space and 256 MB of RAM to be a comfortable minimum. And with the price of disk space below $1 per GB and RAM being between $50 (desktop) and $100 (laptop) per GB, the more the merrier.

Preserving Your Existing Data

If you already have Windows or Linux running on your system, and you want to keep it, you should check out "Dual-Boot Ubuntu and Windows" [Hack #6], which explains how to set up a dual-boot Ubuntu system. However, if you're just interested in archiving your existing installation so that you can pull files off of it at a later time [Hack #7], you have some choices:

New hard drive

Since the cost of storage is so low, you might want to pull and replace your current hard drive. Depending on the age of your current machine, that might give you a modest performance improvement, but it also gives you the opportunity to increase your disk space. Once you've done so, you can install your existing hard drive into an external enclosure so that you can access your old files (and use any free space for extra storage). Another option would be to simply buy an external drive and copy all your files onto it before you install Ubuntu.

Burn it to optical media

If your files can fit, burn them to CD or DVD for safekeeping. Linux will be able to read practically any format that you can put on an optical disc if you want to retrieve these files later.

Shrink your existing partition

If you want your data at your fingertips, then you should spend some time deleting everything you can live without from your old operating system: applications, datafiles, etc. If you're running Windows, make sure you disable hibernation in the control panel's power settings, because hibernation requires a file equal to the size of your installed RAM. Also, if you're not planning to boot the old operating system on a regular basis, disable the paging file. Do everything you can to free up disk space. Then defragment your drive and shrink the partition using a tool such as Partition Magic (*http://www.symantec.com/partitionmagic/*) or the Ubuntu installer's partitioning tool. If you want your old data at your fingertips and you still want to be able to boot up the old OS, be sure to check out "Dual-Boot Ubuntu and Windows" **[Hack #6]**.

Move the data to another machine

If you've got another computer with lots of storage, copy the files across the network to a safe spot on that computer. Even if you have a wireless network, consider using a network cable for the transfer, since it will run a lot faster that way.

Getting the Installation CD

Before you install Ubuntu, you'll need to choose which flavor you want: Ubuntu, Kubuntu (Ubuntu with KDE as the default desktop), or Edubuntu (Ubuntu designed for young people). Although you can download a different CD-ROM for each one, you can install their core components **[Hack #54]** later; the packages *ubuntu-desktop*, *kubuntu-desktop*, and *edubuntu-desktop* can be installed at any time.

> Another flavor of Ubuntu is Xubuntu (the package *xubuntu-desktop*), available at *https://wiki.ubuntu.com/Xubuntu*, which is a variant of Ubuntu that's optimized for older computers. The desktop system is more lightweight, so it's less demanding in terms of memory, CPU, and video-card resources.

Once you've decided which flavor of Ubuntu you want, go to the Ubuntu (*http://www.ubuntu.com*), Kubuntu (*http://www.kubuntu.org*), or Edubuntu (*http://www.edubuntu.org*) home page and follow the download link. Next, you'll need to choose which mirror site to install from (pick one that's close to you geographically), and then choose Intel x86 (for most PC compatibles), AMD64 (64-bit AMD-based PC compatibles), or PowerPC (for Macs, but if you choose this one, you should be in a different hack **[Hack #8]**).

On the download site, you'll find links that go directly to the CD image, an ISO file that you can burn to a CD-R using your favorite CD-burning utility. Mac OS X includes Disk Utility in the */Applications/Utilities* folder. Linux usually includes the command-line *cdrecord* utility, and, in many cases, there will be a graphical frontend available **[Hack #33]**. Windows does not have its own CD-burning utility, but most PCs come bundled with a CD-burning application.

> Be careful on Windows. I burned a few discs on my Dell 700m that wouldn't boot at all before I figured out what was happening. It turned out that the CD-burning application that Dell so thoughtfully bundled with my computer wouldn't burn bootable ISOs without a paid upgrade. However, there are some free ISO burners for Windows. Microsoft includes a free ISO burner (CDBURN) in its Windows Server 2003 resource kit (*http://www.microsoft.com/downloads/details.aspx?FamilyID=9d467a69-57ff-4ae7-96ee-b18c4790cffd&DisplayLang=en*), which, despite the name, runs on Windows XP. Alex Feinman's ISO Recorder (*http://isorecorder.alexfeinman.com/isorecorder.htm*) is free and works well.

Installing Ubuntu

Most computers will boot from the CD-ROM drive automatically, so put the Ubuntu CD into your computer, shut it down, and reboot. (If you try to insert the Ubuntu CD in the computer while it's booting, there's a good chance that whatever's on your hard drive will start booting before your computer even knows you've inserted a bootable CD, so press Ctrl-Alt-Delete after you insert the CD). If your computer refuses to boot from the

CD, reboot it and enter the BIOS menu (usually by pressing F2, Del, or Escape as the computer is starting). Navigate through the BIOS menu and look for a set of boot options, and make sure that the CD-ROM is configured at a higher priority than your hard drive (it should be the first or, if you have a floppy drive, the second item in the list). If in doubt, consult the manual that came with your motherboard or your PC. If you don't have that manual, you should be able to download it in HTML or PDF form from the manufacturer's web site.

> In very rare cases, you may have a computer that can't boot from CD-ROM. I had an ultraportable Sharp Actius MM10 that came with an external CD-ROM drive. It worked great until I tried to boot from a Linux install CD. It turned out that the CD-ROM drive was defective, and Sharp exchanged it for a working one. However, if you're in this situation, you may not have to wait for a new drive to arrive: instead, you could boot over the network [Hack #11] to install Ubuntu on your computer.

When you boot from the CD, you'll be offered several Install options: to the hard disk, OEM mode, or server. If you choose Install to the Hard Disk, you'll go through the standard Ubuntu install. OEM mode is good if you're setting up a computer that someone else will use, since it lets you set up all the hardware configuration and choose software packages, but lets the user do all the personalization (choosing a username, picking her preferred language, etc.). The server installation will set up a minimal Ubuntu system; if you want to add a desktop environment later, you can install *ubuntu-desktop*, *kubuntu-desktop*, *edubuntu-desktop*, or *xubuntu-desktop* when the need arises.

Before you start the installation, you can press F3 to choose the video mode to use, F4 to enable some assistive features, F5 to allow you to edit the boot-time kernel arguments and to enable some more options (including keyboard map and expert mode). Once you've made your choices (or left everything at the defaults), press Enter to start the installation. During the installation, you'll go through the following steps (in expert mode, you'll be taken to a main menu between each step):

Choose Language
    In this step, you'll choose the default language for your system.

Choose Locale
    This lets you select which locale or locales to install on your system. The *locale* is a feature that works in conjunction with the language to control such things as alphabetic sort order and the way dates and numbers are displayed.

Select a Keyboard Layout

This is where you choose the type of keyboard connected to your system.

Detect CD-ROM

By default, this step won't prompt you unless it has a problem finding your CD-ROM. In expert mode, you'll get to review and customize the installer's decision. You'll also be prompted to enable PCMCIA/PC Card services in expert mode during this stage.

Load Installer Components from CD

As with the previous step, the installer won't bug you unless it has a problem here. In expert mode, it will offer some extra components.

Detect Network Hardware

In this step, you get to choose which network adapter to use. In expert mode, it will offer some extra options.

Configure the Network

By default, the Ubuntu installer will attempt to configure the network using DHCP. If it fails, it will offer you some options to configure it differently. In expert mode, you'll be able to configure the network manually. Once the network is configured, you'll be prompted for a hostname (the default will be *ubuntu*, unless the installer finds an existing installation, in which case it will determine the hostname from that). In expert mode, you'll also be prompted for a domain name.

Choose a Mirror

In expert mode, this step lets you choose which mirror to use for additional components and package repositories. In regular mode, you'll be prompted to supply only an HTTP proxy, a server that makes requests to web servers on your behalf (usually found only on corporate or campus networks; leave it blank if you don't use one).

Detect Disks

In this step, the Ubuntu installer will detect hard disks. In expert mode, you will be prompted for some additional options, but normally this will run without any intervention.

Partition Disks

At this stage, the Ubuntu installer will offer some choices: resize your existing partition and use the free space, erase the entire disk, or manually edit the partition table. You'll notice that there are two ways you can erase the entire disk: just using the disk (usually something like "Erase entire disk: IDE1") or creating a logical volume ("Erase entire disk and use LVM"). Logical volumes offer advanced features, such as the ability to dynamically reallocate disk space between partitions.

If you want to keep your existing operating system, choose the resize option. If you want to wipe out the entire disk and put Ubuntu on it, choose one of the other options (the basic "Erase entire disk" option is a good choice if you are unsure).

Confirm Partitioning

This is the point of no return, so the Ubuntu installer reviews the partitioning choices you've made and asks you to confirm them. If you say Yes here, it will repartition your machine, possibly destroying existing data if you've chosen to remove or replace an existing partition.

Configure the Time Zone

In this step, you'll need to choose your time zone.

Configure the Clock

The Ubuntu installer needs to know how your clock is configured. Most computers have a clock that's set to the local time, but Ubuntu lets you configure it so it's set to Coordinated Universal Time (UTC). The choice here is not terribly important unless you plan to dual-boot between Ubuntu and Windows, in which case you should not set the clock to UTC.

Set Up Users and Passwords

At this point, you'll be able to add a user to the system. If you are in expert mode, you'll have some additional options, including the ability to create a password for the *root* user (by default, Ubuntu expects you to use the *sudo* command to use programs that require *root* privileges).

Install the Base System

This step will run without your intervention unless there is a problem. The installer will put a base installation of Ubuntu onto your system at this point. In expert mode, you'll have the opportunity to choose which kernel image to install.

Configure apt

This step is one of those points when it's a good idea to have a network connection, since the installer will try to contact the Ubuntu mirrors to verify that they are reachable. If it can't, it won't add them to the configuration file (*/etc/apt/sources.list*). In expert mode, you'll be asked some additional questions.

Select and Install Software

This step installs the rest of Ubuntu, including the GNOME (or KDE) desktop, and can take quite a while. Despite the name of the step, you won't be asked to choose which packages are installed. However, you will be prompted to select which video modes to use with the X server.

Copy Remaining Packages to Hard Disk

This step is offered in expert mode and gives you the option to copy 400 MB of packages to your hard drive, which eliminates the need to keep the CD-ROM handy.

Install the Boot Loader on a Hard Disk

This installs the GRUB boot loader on your hard drive. You'll be able to choose the LILO boot loader instead if you are in expert mode. Either LILO or GRUB is capable of booting Ubuntu, but GRUB is more flexible and easier to configure. In expert mode, you'll also be given the opportunity to select a password for your boot loader.

Finish the Installation

This step writes configurations to your new Ubuntu install and reboots you into your new Ubuntu system.

Once you've got Ubuntu up and running, you can log in as the user you created during setup, and start exploring your desktop, whether it be GNOME [Hack #15] or KDE [Hack #16].

—Brian Jepson

Dual-Boot Ubuntu and Windows

HACK #6

If you're not ready to give Ubuntu total control over your computer, you can meet it halfway. Learn how to install Ubuntu so you can dual-boot with Windows, even if Windows already owns your entire hard drive.

"Install Ubuntu" [Hack #5] details how to install Ubuntu Linux on your machine as the primary operating system. But what if you're not ready to ditch Windows, or you've got a business requirement to run a certain Windows-only application? A possible solution for you might be to enable your system to dual-boot both Windows and Ubuntu. A dual-boot system has multiple hard disk partitions or hard disks, with each partition or disk containing a complete operating system. Typically, there is a boot loader installed on the first hard disk in the system that lets you choose which operating system to boot when you power on the system.

The Dapper Drake version of Ubuntu supports setting up a dual-boot environment from within the installer. Previous versions also had this capability; however, Dapper's installer automatically shrinks your current Windows partition and makes space available for the Ubuntu installation. Prior to this feature, you had to manually shrink your current Windows partition using tools like PartitionMagic or qtparted.

Preparation

There are just a couple of preparation steps that must be taken prior to setting up a dual-boot system:

- Your current Windows partition must be freshly defragmented to ensure that there is a large, contiguous block of free space available to dedicate to Ubuntu.

>   There are some files that the Windows defragmentation utility can't move, so you may want to try a third-party defragmentation utility, such as Executive Software's Diskeeper (*http://www.diskeeper.com/defrag.asp*). However, if it's your swap (paging) file that refuses to budge, and you have sufficient memory to run without one, try disabling it (right-click My Computer, choose Properties, select Advanced → Performance → Settings → Advanced → Change, and choose No Paging File), defragmenting your hard drive using the Windows disk defragmenter, and then re-enabling the paging file.

- You must back up any critical data you have on your Windows partition. The Ubuntu installer tries to resize your partition as safely as it can, but like any other disk utility, there is a slim chance of a loss of data. Play it safe and back up anything you can't live without.

Installation

Let's get started on the dual-boot installation. (Something to remember is that the dual-boot installation is almost like a standard installation; the major difference lies in the method the partitioner uses to partition the hard disk.) First, boot from the CD, just like a standard standalone Ubuntu install. From the installer screen (see Figure 1-1), select "Install to the hard disk," and press Enter. The installer will kick off and begin the installation.

You'll follow the standard installation procedure [Hack #5], up to the point when the system will ask you how you want your disk partitioned. Rather than selecting "Erase entire disk," you'll select "Resize IDE1 master, partition #1 (hda1) and use freed space," as shown in Figure 1-2.

At this point, the partitioner will ask you how much space you wish to devote to Linux. Input your desired Linux partition size in either percent or gigabytes and select Continue (see Figure 1-3).

The partitioner will then ask you to confirm your decisions, and then it will write the changes to disk. If all looks good, select Yes to proceed, as shown in Figure 1-4.

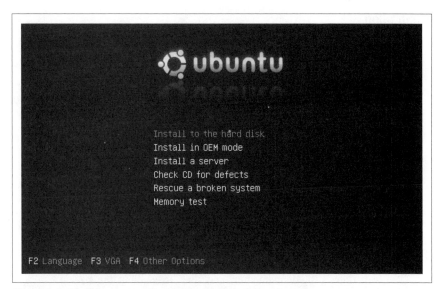

Figure 1-1. The Ubuntu installer, beginning a dual-boot install

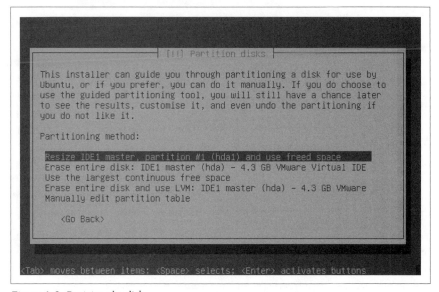

Figure 1-2. Resizing the disk

After this, the installer will actually partition the disk and format your new Linux partition as an *ext3* filesystem, and then you'll be asked to enter your full name to create your Ubuntu account. From this point on, there is no difference between the dual-boot installation and a standard installation. The

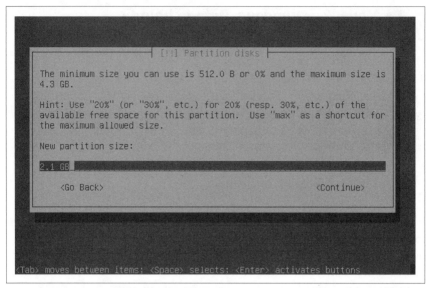

Figure 1-3. Assigning the free space to Linux

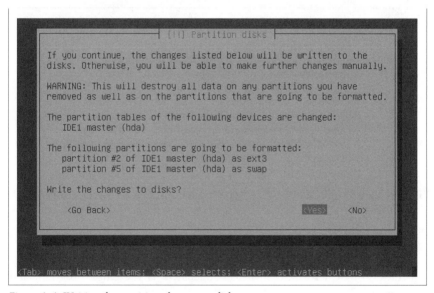

Figure 1-4. Writing the partition changes to disk

system will begin copying the binaries and other data from the CD-ROM, and at the end of the install, the GRUB boot loader will be written to the master boot record. The installer will prompt you to reboot, and you'll be able to select from Windows or Linux at boot time.

Move Your Windows Data to Ubuntu

Your files, bookmarks, and other settings are locked away in a Windows
installation. Learn how to move them over to your new Ubuntu system.

So you're making the big move. You're ready to pack everything up and
move from Windows to Ubuntu. The easy part is getting Ubuntu up and
running. The trickier part is migrating all your data, which is spread out all
over your Windows hard disk. Here's how to pack up all your stuff and
make use of it on your new Ubuntu system.

Make Sure You Notify the Post Office

If you're switching from Outlook, you probably won't be able to directly
import your mail settings into a Linux mail program. Your best bet is to
install Thunderbird (*http://www.mozilla.com/thunderbird/*) on your Windows machine and import all your Outlook settings into Thunderbird. Once
you've done that, you'll more easily be able to export your mail and contacts into formats that Linux mail programs can understand.

> If your mail account is on an IMAP server, you won't need to
> worry about all this exporting and importing. Since IMAP
> keeps the mail on the server, all you need to do is configure
> your new mail client with your email server, login, and pass-
> word information, and all your mail (your inbox and email
> folders) will appear on the new system. Because IMAP keeps
> everything on the server, you can access the same email
> account from multiple servers, and you'll always have the
> same email messages on each computer. However, if you've
> moved any mail into local folders, you will need to export
> and import it.

Transfer Outlook into Thunderbird. Before you transfer your Outlook email
into Thunderbird, first make sure that Outlook is set to be the default mail
application (if you've been using it for your mail application, it probably is).
Open the Control Panel and double-click on Internet Options. Go to the
Programs tab and make sure that Microsoft Outlook (or Outlook Express,
depending on which one you use) is specified as the email program, and
then click OK.

Next, launch Mozilla Thunderbird. Select No when it asks whether you
want to make Thunderbird your default email application. If this is the first
time you've run it, it will prompt you to import your mail and settings.

If not, select Import from the Tools menu. Now you're ready to import your
mail. When the Import dialog box appears, select Mail and click Next.

Choose Outlook or Outlook Express and click Next. When it's done, click Finish. Your mail is now sitting in Thunderbird.

Transfer your Thunderbird mail to Ubuntu. If you transferred your mail from Outlook, it will be sitting in a Local Folder called Outlook Mail. You should have a few folders there, including Deleted Items, Drafts, Inbox, Outbox, and Sent Items. If you expected a whole bunch of mail to be imported from Outlook but found nothing, check to see whether you are using IMAP for your email (see the earlier note about transferring your IMAP account).

To grab the mail folders from Thunderbird, you'll need to locate your *profile folder*. First, shut down Thunderbird, and then open a Windows Command Prompt. Next, change to your Thunderbird directory with this command:

```
cd %APPDATA%\Thunderbird
```

(APPDATA is a Windows environment variable that points to the currently logged-in user's *Application Data* directory.) You'll find a *Profiles* directory in there, and in that directory, there should be a directory with a funny name, such as *pr4qpneu.default*. This is your Thunderbird profile directory. In this directory, look for the subdirectory *Mail\Local Folders*, and then look for your mail folders, which may be in yet another subdirectory.

For example, this directory contains some empty folders (such as *Drafts*, *Sent*, and *Trash*):

```
C:\... \Local Folders> dir
 Volume in drive C has no label.
 Volume Serial Number is 864B-4AB0

 Directory of C:\Documents and Settings\bjepson\Application
 Data\Thunderbird\Profiles\pr4qpneu.default\Mail\Local Folders

03/12/2006  04:24 PM    <DIR>          .
03/12/2006  04:24 PM    <DIR>          ..
10/04/2005  05:11 PM                 0 Drafts
03/12/2006  03:07 PM             1,445 Drafts.msf
10/04/2005  06:36 PM             1,236 Junk.msf
03/12/2006  04:24 PM                27 msgFilterRules.dat
03/12/2006  04:24 PM                 0 Outlook Mail
03/12/2006  05:17 PM             1,185 Outlook Mail.msf
03/12/2006  04:29 PM    <DIR>          Outlook Mail.sbd
10/04/2005  05:11 PM                 0 Sent
03/12/2006  03:07 PM             1,443 Sent.msf
10/04/2005  06:36 PM             1,320 Templates.msf
03/12/2006  04:24 PM                 0 Trash
03/12/2006  05:17 PM             1,448 Trash.msf
10/04/2005  05:11 PM                 0 Unsent Messages
03/12/2006  03:07 PM             1,797 Unsent Messages.msf
              13 File(s)          9,901 bytes
         3 Dir(s)  67,812,487,168 bytes free
```

But the imported Outlook folders are in the *Outlook Mail.sbd* subdirectory, including a 13 MB *Inbox* folder (these are the files you want to copy over to your Linux system):

```
C:\... \Local Folders> dir "Outlook Mail.sbd"
 Volume in drive C has no label.
 Volume Serial Number is 864B-4AB0

 Directory of C:\Documents and Settings\bjepson\Application
 Data\Thunderbird\Profiles\pr4qpneu.default\Mail\Local
 Folders\Outlook Mail.sbd

03/12/2006  04:29 PM    <DIR>          .
03/12/2006  04:29 PM    <DIR>          ..
03/12/2006  04:24 PM                 0 Deleted Items
03/12/2006  04:24 PM             1,212 Deleted Items.msf
03/12/2006  04:24 PM                 0 Drafts
03/12/2006  04:24 PM             1,205 Drafts.msf
03/12/2006  04:24 PM        13,094,192 Inbox
03/12/2006  04:44 PM            79,534 Inbox.msf
03/12/2006  04:24 PM                 0 Outbox
03/12/2006  04:24 PM             1,205 Outbox.msf
03/12/2006  04:24 PM                 0 Sent Items
03/12/2006  04:24 PM             1,209 Sent Items.msf
              10 File(s)     13,178,557 bytes
               2 Dir(s)  67,812,483,072 bytes free
```

These folders use the Unix mbox format and can be imported into most Ubuntu email programs. For example, you can basically reverse the process to move the folder from Thunderbird on Windows to Thunderbird on Linux: find your *Local Folders* directory in your Ubuntu *~/.mozilla-thunderbird* directory, make sure that Thunderbird is not running, and copy the files into that directory. When you restart Thunderbird, the folders you copied should appear in your list of Local Folders.

In Evolution, you can select File → Import to bring up the Evolution Import Assistant. When prompted to choose the Importer Type, select Import a Single File and then specify the mbox file when prompted to choose a file. If you have trouble importing files into Evolution, you can copy them manually: exit out of Evolution, and copy the files to *~/.evolution/mail/local*.

If you have any problems, check the MozillaZine article on importing and exporting mail at *http://kb.mozillazine.org/Importing_and_exporting_your_mail*. However, considering how complicated it is to move mail from one system to another, you should consider using IMAP, which eliminates all these steps the next time you need to move from one machine to another; with IMAP, all your mail and folders are stored on the server. Contact your system administrator, Internet Service Provider, or mail provider to find out whether they support IMAP.

Are You Bringing the Browser?

You'll be happy to hear that exporting and importing your browser settings will be simple compared to migrating email. If you're using Internet Explorer, you'll first need to export your cookies and bookmarks and then copy them over to your Ubuntu system. To export them, start Internet Explorer, and select File → Import and Export. This starts the Import/Export Wizard. You'll have to run it twice: once for your cookies and once for your favorites (bookmarks).

If you're using Firefox on your old system, you can locate your profile folder and grab the *bookmarks.html* and *cookies.txt* files. To find your Firefox profile directory, open up a Windows Command Prompt and issue this command:

```
cd %APPDATA%\Mozilla\Firefox\Profiles
```

As with Thunderbird, you'll find a strangely named directory, such as *9yk75acu.default*. Your cookies and bookmarks will be sitting in this directory.

Once you've grabbed your cookies and bookmarks, you can use your browser's import function to bring them over to Ubuntu. For example, with Firefox, you can import bookmarks by selecting Bookmarks → Manage Bookmarks, and then selecting File → Import. To copy your cookies over, you'll first need to close Firefox, then paste the contents of the exported cookies into your existing *cookies.txt* file in your Firefox profile directory on your Ubuntu system, located in *~/.mozilla/firefox*.

 Cookies that you've exported from Internet Explorer are a bit more complex: you'll need to edit the *cookies.txt* file and put a period before every cookie that begins with a domain name. For more information, see *http://kb.mozillazine.org/ Import_cookies*.

Your Stuff, Your Music

Unless you've decided to put your documents elsewhere, Windows makes moving them to Ubuntu quite easy. Windows uses the *My Documents* folder to organize your documents—including music, video, and others—and most applications respect this organization (for example, iTunes organizes its files under *My Documents\My Music\iTunes*). The actual location of the *My Documents* folder varies by Windows version. For example, on Windows XP, it is on the system drive (usually C:) in *\Documents and Settings\ <username>\My Documents*.

Although it's easy to copy over the files, some files, such as multimedia files, will probably not play on Ubuntu without a little extra effort. See Chapter 3 for more information.

Your Little Black Book

To move your appointments and contacts over, it's best if you can get your data into the vCalendar or iCalendar format (for calendars) and the VCard format (for contacts). If you can do this, it will be simple to import into an application such as Evolution or Thunderbird.

Outlook will let you export items one at a time, but this is too tedious for importing many contacts or calendar items. The free OutPod (*http://outpod. stoer.de/*) is designed to export Outlook items to an iPod, but to accomplish this, it uses the vCalendar and iCalendar formats to store the data. To use it, simply run *OutPod.exe* and navigate to your list of calendar items or contacts (Outlook will probably ask for your permission to let OutPod access its data). Click in the list of contacts or calendars and press Ctrl-A to select all. Then click OutPod's Outlook menu and choose "Save Selected Items in One File."

Copy the *.vcf* (VCard), *.ics* (iCalendar), or *.vcs* (VCalendar) file over to your Ubuntu system, and import it into Evolution or Thunderbird (addresses only). For Evolution, choose File → Import to bring up the Evolution Import Assistant, and choose to Import a Single File when prompted. Select the file you want to import (you may need to specify the file type), as shown in Figure 1-5, and then continue through the Import Assistant to import the data.

Another utility you may find useful for exporting calendars from Outlook is the free Outlook to iCal Export Utility (*http://outlook2ical.sourceforge.net*).

If you're using Thunderbird on Windows, you can export contacts using the LDAP Data Interchange Format (*.ldif*). On your Windows machine, launch Thunderbird, select Tools → Address Book to bring up your list of contacts, and then select Tools → Export to export all contacts. When the Save As dialog appears, choose LDIF. You'll be able to import LDIF into Thunderbird and Evolution.

Am I Forgetting Anything?

As a last check, open up your Windows Control Panel, go to Add/Remove Programs, and review the list of programs. Do you see any that store their data in a nonstandard location? For example, anything with a keychain,

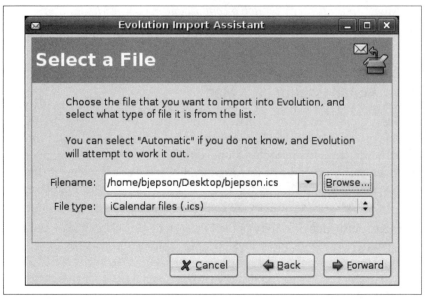

Figure 1-5. Importing an iCalendar file

such as GNU Privacy Guard or the PuTTY SSH suite, might be keeping some keys you can't live without.

GNU Privacy Guard keeps its files in the *gnupg* subdirectory of the user's *Application Data* folder. APPDATA is an environment variable that expands to the user's *Application Data* directory, so issuing the command:

```
dir %APPDATA%
```

in a Windows Command Prompt will reveal *gnupg*'s location. PuTTY keeps its keys wherever you decided to put them. If you've been using Pageant, select Add Key, and it should pop up with an Open File dialog set to the most recent directory you used.

If you're a Cygwin (*http://www.cygwin.com*) fan, don't forget that it keeps its home directories in a separate location (usually *C:\cygwin\home*). You may have all kinds of important documents and dotfiles kicking around there!

You Could Just Hire a Mover

There are a few third-party applications available to help move from Windows to Linux, but not all of them support Ubuntu. If you have a lot of machines to migrate, you might want to check out one of these:

- Desktop Migration Agent (*http://www.alacos.com/linux.html*)
- Progression Desktop (*http://www.versora.com/*)

- MoveOver (*http://www.resolvo.com/products/moveover/index.htm*)
- LSP (*http://www.das.com.tw/elsp.htm*)

—Brian Jepson

HACK #8 Install Ubuntu on a Mac

Install Ubuntu and Mac OS X on the same machine for the best of both worlds.

Apple hardware has some quirks and differences compared to normal PC machines, but is generally of very high quality and can make a great Ubuntu machine. And with a little extra work, you can set it up to dual-boot for those times you still need to use Mac OS X.

First, get your hands on a copy of the PPC installer for Ubuntu. You can find instructions on downloading and burning Ubuntu disk images in "Install Ubuntu" [Hack #5].

Reinstall Mac OS X

If you want to run your computer dual-boot with both Mac OS X and Ubuntu installed at the same time, you will need to reinstall Mac OS X so that you can repartition your disk safely. If you intend to go for a straight Ubuntu system and don't need Mac OS X anymore, you can skip ahead to "Install Ubuntu."

After backing up any documents or data already installed, put the Mac OS X install CD into the CD-ROM drive and reboot. As the computer reboots, hold down the C key to force it to boot from the CD and start the Mac OS X installer. Once the installer loads, you will be presented with a screen to select your preferred language. Don't select a language yet; instead, go to Installer → Open Disk Utility to open the Mac OS X Disk Utility. On the left of Disk Utility is a pane listing disks and volumes, so select the hard disk on which you intend to install Mac OS X and Linux. Next, click the Partition tab at the top of the right pane. Under Volume Scheme, click the drop-down menu labeled Current and select "2 Partitions." The first partition is going to become your Ubuntu partition, and the second will be used by Mac OS X, so click the central divider between the partitions and drag it to adjust the relative partition sizes to suit your requirements, keeping in mind that Mac OS X requires a minimum of 1.5 GB to install.

Next, click the second partition and select Mac OS Extended (Journaled) as the format. The format of the first partition doesn't matter because you'll be replacing it anyway when Ubuntu is installed.

Once you are happy with the settings, click the Partition button near the bottom right and confirm that you want to go ahead. This step will delete all the files on the hard drive.

Once the partitioning is complete, select Disk Utility → Quit Disk Utility to return to the language-selection screen. Click Continue and follow the usual Mac OS X installation steps until you get to Select Destination, at which point you will have two partitions to choose from. Select the second and proceed with the rest of the Mac OS X installation.

Install Ubuntu

Put the Ubuntu PPC install disk in the CD-ROM drive and (re)start your computer, holding down the C key as the machine boots to force it to start up from the CD. Follow the usual installation prompts until you get to disk partitioning. If you want to erase everything on your hard drive and replace it with Ubuntu, you can select Erase Entire Disk. Otherwise, select "Manually edit partition table" to view the partitions created by Mac OS X. This is where you'll probably get a bit of a shock, because you'll discover that Mac OS X didn't just create two partitions as it claimed—it probably created about 10. Most of them will be very small partitions that are used by the OS as part of the boot process, so you need to leave them alone, but you should also see the large partition you left aside for Ubuntu during the Mac OS X installation process. It will most likely be marked as an "hfs+" partition, so select it and press Enter. Arrow down to "Delete the partition" and press Enter, and you will then be returned to the partition table, which will now have a large area marked FREE SPACE.

At this point, you could create the partitions you need manually, but the Mac OS bootloader has some unusual requirements, so it's simplest to let the installer figure things out for itself. Select "Guided partitioning," and this time select "Use the largest contiguous free space" to have three new partitions created for you: one for the bootloader, one as your root partition, and one as swap.

Select "Finish partitioning and write changes to disk," press Enter to proceed, and, if the summary screen shows the changes you expected, select Yes. This is the point of no return when the disk is changed, so make sure you're happy with what is being done.

The installer will then create filesystems in the new partitions and continue with the regular Ubuntu installation with questions about your location and setting up an initial user.

Once the installer has finished, you will be asked to remove the install CD and restart.

When your Mac restarts, you will see a yaboot menu giving three options: press L or wait to boot Linux, press X to boot Mac OS X, or press C to boot from CD-ROM. The X option takes you straight to the regular Mac OS X startup process, while the L option takes you to another yaboot menu where you can type in boot options. Just press Enter to begin the Ubuntu startup process.

For the most part, everything should work smoothly. However, if you have an AirPort Extreme card, it may not be supported well by Ubuntu. One option is to simply use an Ethernet cable, or to install a PCI, PC Card, or USB Wi-Fi adapter that is supported by Ubuntu. You may also want to look into the Broadcom 43xx Linux Driver (*http://bcm43xx.berlios.de/*), which is an open source driver for the chipset used in most, if not all, AirPort Extreme cards.

Set Up Your Printer
HACK #9 Get that printer connected, up, and running with Ubuntu.

Ubuntu uses CUPS, the Common Unix Printing System, to manage printers and print queues. CUPS can be configured using a variety of tools, including the GNOME CUPS Manager and its own built-in web interface that runs on port 631.

GNOME CUPS Manager

To launch GNOME CUPS Manager, select System → Administration → Printing, which will display a list of currently installed printers, shown in Figure 1-6, and give you the option of adding a new printer.

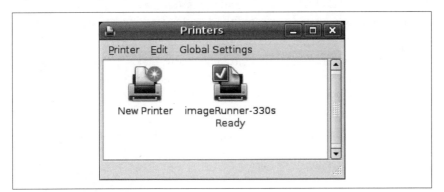

Figure 1-6. GNOME CUPS Manager

Double-click the New Printer icon to open the "Add a Printer" window. Here, you need to specify whether your printer is connected directly to your computer or is on your network (see Figure 1-7). If your printer is connected by USB, it's a good idea to use the instructions in "Mount Removable Devices with Persistent Names" [Hack #83] to assign a permanent name to your printer before going any further; otherwise, it will probably be assigned a different bus ID every time you plug it in, and you will be asked to configure it again each time!

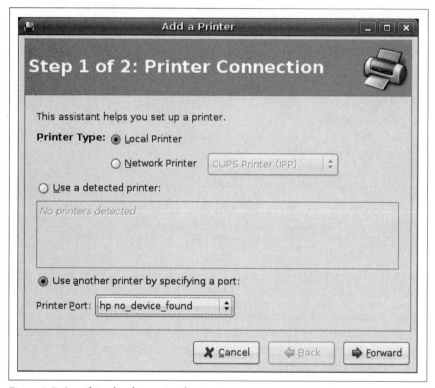

Figure 1-7. Specifying local or network printer

If your printer is connected via the network, you will need to specify the protocol: IPP (Internet Printing Protocol), SMB (Windows printer sharing), LPD (Line Printer Daemon), or HP JetDirect. Each of those protocols in turn provides a number of configuration options to specify the printer identity. In Figure 1-8, the printer is connected to the second port on a network print server using IPP.

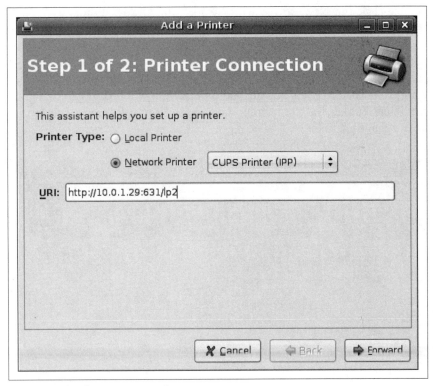

Figure 1-8. Configuring a network printer

Specify the printer manufacturer and then select the model from the pro-vided list, as shown in Figure 1-9.

If your printer model isn't included in the list, you can try using one of the drivers listed under the Generic manufacturer, or, if it's a PostScript printer, you can load the manufacturer's supplied PPD (PostScript Printer Descrip-tion) file using the Install Driver button.

Apply the changes, and you'll return to the list of installed printers with your new printer listed, as shown in Figure 1-10.

CUPS Web Interface

GNOME CUPS Manager provides quick access to basic options, but to really take control of CUPS, you should use the built-in web-management interface. Open your web browser and point it at *http://localhost:631* to see a huge range of options.

Figure 1-9. Selecting a printer model

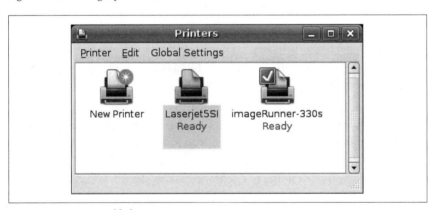

Figure 1-10. Printer added

Share Local Printers

You can allow other computers on your network to print to your locally connected printer by setting the Shared option.

Open */etc/cups/printers.conf* in a text editor to see the definition for your printers. Each printer is defined in a separate block, with configuration options applied in any order inside the block, and you should see an existing configuration option of:

```
Shared no
```

Change this to:

```
Shared yes
```

After you make changes to *printers.conf*, restart the CUPS scheduler:

```
$ sudo /etc/init.d/cupsys restart
```

Apply Print Quotas

CUPS implements a very simple quota system that allows you to restrict page count over a specified period, but it can be applied only per printer and not per user.

Open */etc/cups/printers.conf* in a text editor and add two options: PageLimit, which is the page count limit, and QuotaPeriod, which is the period in seconds for which you want it enforced. To apply a limit of 200 pages per week, you could set those options to:

```
QuotaPeriod 604800
PageLimit 200
```

One day is 86,400 seconds, a week is 604,800 seconds, and a month is 2,592,000 seconds.

You can also apply a KLimit option, which is the amount of data in kilobytes that the printer is allowed to receive. This can be useful if you want to prevent people sending extremely large print jobs to specific printers.

 Remember to restart CUPS after making changes to *printers.conf*.

One possible hack to get around the per-printer limitation of quota settings is to configure the same printer multiple times, each with a different name and access controls but all communicating with the same device. The quota for each "printer" will then be tracked and enforced individually, so you could have each user connecting to a different virtual printer to enforce individual quotas.

Install Ubuntu on an External Drive

HACK #10

You can, in fact, install, boot, and run Ubuntu completely from a FireWire, USB, or other external drive, but it does require some special steps. This hack walks you through the process from start to finish.

In the process of working on this book, we realized one disadvantage to using a laptop as a primary computer: it is much more difficult to swap out hard drives for test systems. We wanted to set up an Ubuntu system so that we could test various hacks on a vanilla install, but we didn't necessarily want to repartition and install on the main laptop hard drive if we didn't have to. The solution was to install and run Ubuntu from an external USB drive we had; that way, the regular system stayed intact but we could boot Ubuntu whenever we wanted.

Unfortunately, this sort of install does not automatically work without some tweaking due to a few different reasons:

- By default, the *initrd* (initial ram disk) file that Ubuntu uses does not contain all of the drivers you need to boot from a removable drive. Your BIOS will find the drive fine (provided it supports booting from removable drives), but once the kernel loads, Linux won't be able to see or mount the drive to continue the boot process.

- Even if the *initrd* has the appropriate drivers, it takes a few seconds for the kernel to load these modules and detect your removable drive before it tries to use it. During this time, the system will likely try to boot and will not be able to find the removable drive because it hasn't finished configuring.

- The Ubuntu installer is very handy in that it tries to detect other OSes you might have installed on the system and will provide GRUB menu entries for each OS. Unfortunately, this means that it will set up any OS you have on the internal hard drive as being on the first BIOS drive, with the removable drive being second (or third or fourth if you have other drives on the system). When the BIOS boots from the removable drive, it will configure it as the first drive on the system, which will confuse GRUB.

In this hack, we discuss how to fix each of these problems so that you can install and boot Ubuntu from a removable drive.

Set Up the Partitions

The first step is to start the Ubuntu install process as you would with any other system, so read through "Install Ubuntu" [Hack #5] until you get to the section about partitioning a drive. When Ubuntu gets to the disk-partitioning

tool, note that by default it will probably pick any internal IDE or SCSI drive currently in the system. If your system uses an IDE drive, you can choose your external drive by selecting the SCSI drive the system has detected. The line will probably refer to a disk called "SCSI (0,0,0) (sda)." If you already have a SCSI hard drive in the system, it will be a bit more difficult to locate the USB drive, but chances are it will be the last SCSI drive on the system.

> Be absolutely sure you pick the correct drive in this phase, because Ubuntu will format and repartition the drive you choose and wipe out any data that might have been there. If you are uncertain which drive is the appropriate one, boot from the Ubuntu Live CD and confirm which device names (*sda*, *sdb*, etc.) it assigns the different drives on your system.

Install GRUB

Once you choose the correct drive to format, continue with the Ubuntu installation process until it gets to the GRUB bootloader stage. Here, you will be asked whether you want to load GRUB to the MBR of the internal hard drive. You *don't* want to do this because it will overwrite any boot-loader you are currently using on the system. Instead, say no and then specify */dev/sda* (or whatever Linux device was assigned to your removable drive) in the next screen that appears in order to install GRUB directly on the removable drive.

Use chroot

Next, complete the Ubuntu installation up until when it prompts you to select Continue to reboot the system. Before you reboot, you will need to make some tweaks to the system. The Ubuntu installer actually provides a basic console you can use to run a few limited commands on the system. Hit Alt-F2 to switch to this console, and then hit Enter to activate it.

Now you need to prepare the removable disk so that you can chroot into it and change some files. The removable drive will actually be mounted under the */target* directory, and the first step is to mount the special */proc* filesystem within that drive:

```
# mount -t proc /target/proc
```

Now you can use the *chroot* tool to turn the */target* directory into the effective / partition on the system. This way, you can run commands as though you had booted off of that drive:

```
# chroot /target
```

Tweak initrd

Once inside the *chroot* environment, the first thing to do is to add the modules Linux uses to make your removable drive accessible to the *initrd*. The */etc/mkinitramfs/modules* file lets you configure extra modules to add to an *initrd*, so use your preferred console text editor to edit this file. If you don't have a preferred console text editor, just use *vim* (if you are unfamiliar with *vim*, check out "Edit Configuration Files" [Hack #74] for a *vim* primer):

```
# vim /etc/mkinitramfs/modules
```

Once this file is opened, move to the very bottom of the file and add the following lines and then save and close the file:

```
ehci-hcd
usb-storage
scsi_mod
sd_mod
```

> If your removable drive is connected via IEEE1394, also add the following lines:
>
> ```
> ieee1394
> ohci1394
> sbp2
> ```
>
> and for any other devices, simply add the modules they need to this file.

With the correct modules configured, the next step is to set up a *initrd* so that it will wait a number of seconds before continuing to boot. That way, Linux has time to detect and configure the removable drive. Open */etc/mkinitramfs/initramfs.conf* in a text editor:

```
# vim /etc/mkinitramfs/initramfs.conf
```

Now add a new configuration option to the very top of the file so that Linux will wait for a few seconds before finishing the boot process:

```
WAIT=10
```

In our experience, 10 seconds is enough time for Linux to load a USB drive, but feel free to change this to a longer or shorter value if you need to. Save your changes and close the file.

Now you are ready to re-create an *initrd* file that incorporates the new settings using the *mkinitramfs* tool:

```
# mkinitramfs -o /boot/initrd.img-2.6.15-16-386 /lib/modules/2.6.15-16-386
```

Change the *initrd.img* and */lib/modules* paths to match the kernel version included in your Ubuntu install CD.

Update GRUB

The final step is to change a few settings in the GRUB configuration file. The Ubuntu installer sets up the external device as (hd1) (or second BIOS drive), but you need to change that to (hd0) because the drive will be the first BIOS drive in the system when the BIOS boots from it. Open the GRUB *menu.lst* file with a text editor:

```
# vim /boot/grub/menu.lst
```

and find the lines that refer to the GRUB root device. They will look something like the following:

```
## default grub root device
## e.g. groot=(hd0,0)
# groot=(hd1,0)
```

Change the last line to refer to hd0 instead:

```
## default grub root device
## e.g. groot=(hd0,0)
# groot=(hd0,0)
```

Next, find the section in the file that refers to different Ubuntu kernels. It should look something like the following:

```
title       Ubuntu, kernel 2.6.15-16-386
root        (hd1,0)
kernel      /boot/vmlinuz-2.6.15-16-386 root=/dev/sda1 ro quiet splash
initrd      /boot/initrd.img-2.6.15-16-386
boot

title       Ubuntu, kernel 2.6.15-16-386 (recovery mode)
root        (hd1,0)
kernel      /boot/vmlinuz-2.6.15-16-386 root=/dev/sda1 ro single
initrd      /boot/initrd.img-2.6.15-16-386
boot

title       Ubuntu, memtest86+
root        (hd1,0)
kernel      /boot/memtest86+.bin
boot
```

Now change all of the references to hd1 to hd0:

```
title       Ubuntu, kernel 2.6.15-16-386
root        (hd0,0)
kernel      /boot/vmlinuz-2.6.15-16-386 root=/dev/sda1 ro quiet splash
initrd      /boot/initrd.img-2.6.15-16-386
boot

title       Ubuntu, kernel 2.6.15-16-386 (recovery mode)
root        (hd0,0)
kernel      /boot/vmlinuz-2.6.15-16-386 root=/dev/sda1 ro single
```

```
initrd      /boot/initrd.img-2.6.15-16-386
boot

title       Ubuntu, memtest86+
root        (hd0,0)
kernel      /boot/memtest86+.bin
boot
```

If Ubuntu has detected and configured other OSes and you want to be able to choose them as well, simply repeat the same changes to the *root* config option for each OS—only change hd0 to hd1. Then save your changes and close the file.

Now you can leave the chroot environment, so type exit in the console and then hit Alt-F1 to return to the main Ubuntu install console. Now you can select Continue to reboot the machine into your new install.

> Keep in mind that most computers won't boot from a removable drive by default if a CD-ROM or other hard drive is present. Some BIOSes let you configure which device to boot from via a special key at boot time (such as F12). In other BIOSes, you may have to hit Esc, F2, or Del to enter the BIOS and configure the boot device order.

Install from a Network Boot Server

HACK #11

Boot your computer directly off a network server and install Ubuntu without using a CD.

Most modern computers can search the network for a boot server and load the operating system from it without using a local hard disk. This feature is typically used to boot thin clients that may not contain a hard disk at all, but you can also use it as a clever way to start the Ubuntu installation process without needing an install CD. This hack is perfect if you want to install Ubuntu onto a subnotebook with no CD-ROM drive or need to set up a large number of computers for a cluster, lab, or server farm.

Prepare the PXE Boot Server

The first step is to prepare the PXE boot server that will dish up the Ubuntu install image to your client. The easiest way to set this up is with an existing Linux server you have kicking around.

This boot server stores the install image and provides DHCP and TFTP (trivial FTP) services so that computers on the network can find and load the image when they start up. The whole process is triggered by the client connecting to the DHCP server and receiving special instructions telling it to

fetch its boot image from the TFTP server instead of from the local hard disk.

Configure DHCP. If you don't already have a DHCP server on your network, start by installing the *dhcp-server* package on the machine that will be your PXE Boot server:

```
$ sudo apt-get install dhcp-server
```

Then edit */etc/dhcp3/dhcpd/dhcpd.conf* and add a stanza similar to this:

```
host pxeinstall {
  hardware ethernet 00:00:00:00:00:00:00;
  filename "pxelinux.0";
}
```

Substitute the hardware MAC address of your client's Ethernet card in place of the string of zeros. Strictly speaking, you don't need the hardware line at all, but if you include it, your DHCP server will serve up the boot image only to that specific machine, so you won't need to worry about other random machines picking it up and reinstalling Ubuntu over their existing systems. On the other hand, if you're going to do installs on a lot of machines, you can just leave out that line, and every machine that netboots will be able to run the installer. Once you have updated the config restart the DHCP server:

```
$ sudo /otc/init.d/dhcpd restart
```

Configure TFTP. Install a TFTP server:

```
$ sudo apt-get install tftpd-hpa
```

Check */etc/inetd.conf* and make sure it has a line like this:

```
tftp   dgram   udp    wait    root   /usr/sbin/in.tftpd /usr/sbin/in.tftpd ↵
-s /var/lib/tftpboot
```

Next, restart *inetd*:

```
$ sudo /etc/init.d/inetd restart
```

Now you need to fetch the *netboot* install image (type the following all on one line):

```
$ sudo lftp -c "open http://archive.ubuntu.com/ubuntu/dists/dapper/main/
installer-i386/current/images/; mirror netboot/"
```

You will then have a directory called *netboot* with a number of files in it that need to be placed where the TFTP server can find them. The *inetd* config line listed earlier shows the path that *tftp-hpa* uses to store boot images—typically */var/lib/tftpboot*—so copy the files there and extract the boot image:

```
$ sudo cp -a netboot/* /var/lib/tftpboot
$ sudo cd /var/lib/tftpboot
$ sudo tar zxf netboot.tar.gz
```

You can even use a Windows machine as the boot server by installing a TFTP package such as Tftpd32 and placing the Ubuntu install image into the TFTP server root directory. Tftpd32 also includes a built-in DHCP server that you can use to specify the name of the install image. You can download Tftpd32 from *http://tftpd32.jounin.net/*.

Setting up a TFTP server is even easier in Mac OS X because *tftp* is already installed. Just run:

```
$ sudo mkdir -p /private/tftpboot; /sbin/service \
  tftp start
```

and put your install image in place. You will, however, need to install and configure a DHCP server yourself unless you're running Mac OS X Server.

Boot the Client

In order to start the install process, your client machine needs to be able to perform a PXE network boot. Most modern machines can do this directly with a BIOS setting, although some older machines may need a special netboot floppy image to start the process.

Start up your client machine, use whatever key sequence is necessary to enter the BIOS setup menu, and locate the setting for boot devices. (The key sequence to enter the BIOS is usually something like F2 or Esc.) Set the first boot device to be PXE Boot, Network Boot, or the equivalent; save and exit the BIOS; and let the machine boot up again.

Some computers will display a boot menu when you press F12, so you can choose the boot device on the fly without having to modify your BIOS setting.

This time, your machine should report that it's looking for a DHCP server before it gets to the stage of trying to boot off the hard disk. After being given an IP address, it will report that it's searching for a PXE boot image. A couple of seconds later, you should see the Ubuntu installer splash screen, and after that, the installation can proceed exactly as normal—except that all packages will be fetched directly from an Ubuntu mirror rather than from a local CD-ROM.

HACK #12 Submit a Bug Report

All software has bugs, and Ubuntu is no exception. Here's how you can help improve Ubuntu by submitting a bug report.

It's an unfortunate rule of computing: all software has bugs. The Ubuntu developers and folks at Canonical have done their best to minimize the amount of bugs and their impact in the latest release of Ubuntu, but they can't catch everything. However, one of the major advantages of open source software is that you have an opportunity to help improve the software by filing a bug. The process of filing a bug is surprisingly easy and, despite the name, can be a rather fun and interactive process.

Getting Ready to File the Bug

Before you actually go ahead and file a bug, you should run through a little checklist to better assist you in the process. The key thing to remember is that every piece of information you can embed in the bug report will help the people fixing your bug. These people may not have the same hardware as you, and there may be other difficulties in reproducing your bug, so every clue you can provide will help them in solving the mystery.

First, figure out what your problem is, in plain language. Ask yourself what's broken and what the proper behavior should be. Also, is there anything the software is doing that it shouldn't be doing? If you can capture logs or output from a terminal, save that information—you can attach it to the bug. If you have knowledge on how to attach a debugger to your process, you may want to include output from that as well. Ensure you've got the package name of the piece of software you're having trouble with. Save all this information so you can have it handy when it's time to file the bug report.

Creating a Malone Account

Ubuntu's method of filing a bug report is via a web-enabled application called Malone (see Figure 1-11). Malone is part of Launchpad (*https:// launchpad.net/malone/*), and the unique thing about Malone compared to other bugtrackers is that Malone tracks not only Ubuntu bugs, but upstream bugs as well as bugs in other distros. This helps to enable another benefit of open source software: the fact that "given enough eyes, all bugs are shallow." In a nutshell, this means that if one distro pinpoints and fixes a bug, all other distros that use Malone can see the fix, and everyone benefits.

On your first visit to Malone, you'll need to create an account for yourself so you can post to the bug database. Simply click on the Log In/Register link in

Figure 1-11. Your first visit to Malone

the upper-righthand corner and follow the instructions to register an account.

> You can search the Malone bug database without creating an account, but posting new information to the database requires an account.

Searching for Your Bug

You've collected your data and created your account: now it's almost time to file your bug. There's just one thing left to do: search for your bug. Yes, that's right: you should always search the bug database for your bug (or one just like it) before you go ahead and create a new one. If you search for a bug with similar symptoms and criteria as your bug, there's a good chance you'll find a bug report already there. You can check and see if the behavior of the bug is the same, if the developers are stalled waiting for a piece of information, or if the bug's already been fixed and a patch is available.

Additionally, if you do see a bug report that resembles your bug, you can add your comments and information to that bug. That will help consolidate things and let the developers know that multiple people are experiencing that issue. Nothing is more frustrating for developers than duplicate bug reports (well, not entirely; poor bug reports are even worse!).

In Figure 1-12, we've searched for a *gnome-power-manager* issue that we happened to run into. As it happened, there was a pre-existing bug already opened, and the developer was awaiting information. We were able to add our own comments to the bug and give the developer some of the information he was looking for. That's open source in action!

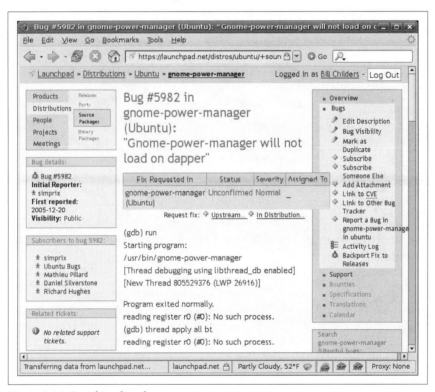

Figure 1-12. Searching for a bug

Filing Your Bug Report

If your bug isn't already in the bug database, then it's time to report it. Log in to Malone if you haven't already, and go to the "Report a bug about a package" page (*https://launchpad.net/malone/bugs/+package*). Select Ubuntu from the drop-down menu and enter the package name in the appropriate field. Next, enter the bug summary. You'll want to be as descriptive as you can in one sentence. Don't say, "gnome-power-manager is broken" or,

worse, "battery icon doesn't work." Either of those two summary lines will ensure that your bug is rejected. A more appropriate summary line would say, "gnome-power-manager icon does not show AC power status."

Next, fill out the description of the problem. Be as objective and descriptive as you can, and include all the notes mentioned earlier. Take your time, and be sure to include every detail. We can't stress enough the importance of including not only what's wrong, but what the software is doing right. Include any debug information you may have gathered.

Once you've done that, you can submit your bug by clicking the Add button. There's a checkbox on the site to keep the contents of the bug confidential, so you'll want to check that box if there's a possible security risk exposed by this bug. However, 99.9 percent of the time the bug won't involve a security risk, and you can safely leave this box unchecked.

Now your bug's filed and in the system! Come back to your bug's page periodically to see if a developer has picked up the problem and made any progress on it.

Use the Command Line

#13

Put your mouse down for a second, pop open a terminal window, and fall in love with the shell all over again.

If you are used to Windows or Mac desktops, the command line might seem like a foreign thing to you. Typing commands into a window might seem, well, arcane. But even though Linux has really progressed on the desktop, there's still a lot of power you can wield at the command line. If this is your first time with a terminal, this hack will guide you through some command-line basics.

> Throughout this book, you'll find a number of places where you'll need to prefix commands with sudo. The *sudo* command [Hack #67] allows you to temporarily execute a command with different user privileges and is frequently used when you need to add or remove software [Hack #54] from the command line.

The first step is to launch a terminal. Click Applications → Accessories → Terminal to start the default GNOME Terminal program.

Navigate the Filesystem

Now that the terminal program is open, you can navigate the filesystem. By default, terminals will open into your home directory, so one thing you

might want to do is see what files are currently in your home directory. The *ls* command displays all the files in the directory you specify (or in the current directory if you don't list a directory):

```
greenfly@ubuntu:~$ ls
Desktop
greenfly@ubuntu:~$ ls Desktop/
screenshot1.png  screenshot2.png
```

The first command lists all of the files in the home directory. In this case, only the *Desktop* directory exists. The second example lists the contents of the *Desktop* directory, where there are two screenshot images.

To change to a different directory, use the *cd* command followed by the directory to change to:

```
greenfly@ubuntu:~$ cd Desktop/
greenfly@ubuntu:~/Desktop$ ls
screenshot1.png  screenshot2.png
```

Notice that the terminal prompt changed in the second line to show that you are currently in the *Desktop* directory. You can also use the *pwd* command to see where you currently are:

```
greenfly@ubuntu:~/Desktop$ pwd
/home/greenfly/Desktop
```

> The ~ symbol is shorthand in Linux for your user's home directory. If you type cd ~ you will automatically change back to your home directory. It saves you from having to type out cd /home/*username*.

Rename and Delete Files and Directories

To create a directory from the command line, type the *mkdir* command followed by the name of the directory to create:

```
greenfly@ubuntu:~$ mkdir test
greenfly@ubuntu:~$ ls
Desktop  test
```

Use the *mv* command to move a file or directory to a different directory, or to rename it in its current directory. To rename the *test* directory you created to *testing*, you can type:

```
greenfly@ubuntu:~$ mv test testing
greenfly@ubuntu:~$ ls
Desktop  testing
```

If you wanted to move the *testing* directory inside the *Desktop* directory, you would just specify the *Desktop* directory as the second argument:

```
greenfly@ubuntu:~$ mv testing Desktop/
greenfly@ubuntu:~$ ls Desktop/
screenshot1.png  screenshot2.png  testing
```

The *rm* command removes files, and *rmdir* removes directories. Just use the commands followed by the files or directories to remove, respectively:

```
greenfly@ubuntu:~$ rm Desktop/screenshot1.png Desktop/screenshot2.png
greenfly@ubuntu:~$ ls Desktop/
testing
greenfly@ubuntu:~$ rmdir Desktop/testing/
greenfly@ubuntu:~$ ls Desktop/
greenfly@ubuntu:~$
```

You can also remove a directory and all files and directories inside of it by running rm -r followed by the name of the directory.

> Be careful when you recursively delete a directory with this command that you do in fact want to remove all of the files within. Once removed via the command line, there's no trash bin to retrieve them from.

File Globs and Tab Completion

There are two major time-savers when dealing with long files on the command line: file globs and tab completion. *File globs* are symbols you can use as wildcards in the place of a filename. You can substitute the ? symbol for any single character in a filename, and * for any number of characters in a filename. For instance, say you had three files: *foo*, *bar*, and *baz*. If you wanted to delete both *bar* and *baz*, you would type:

```
greenfly@ubuntu:$ rm ba?
```

The ? matches both r and the z at the end of the filename. If you wanted to remove all files that started with the letter b, you would type:

```
greenfly@ubuntu:$ rm b*
```

Tab completion is another time-saver on the command line. If you start to type a command and then hit the Tab key, the shell will automatically attempt to complete the name of the command for you. In the case that more than one command matches what you have typed so far, hit Tab an extra time, and you will be shown all of the options that match:

```
greenfly@ubuntu:~$ gnome-cups-<Tab><Tab>
gnome-cups-add      gnome-cups-icon      gnome-cups-manager
```

Tab completion also works for files and directory names. Just type the first part of the filename and hit Tab, and the shell will fill out the rest for you.

Once you are finished with a terminal, you can close the window like any other window, or, alternatively, you can type exit on the command line.

HACK #14 Get Productive with Applications

Even the coolest OS is useless without programs to run on it. Ubuntu ships with lots of built-in applications, including many Linux-based counterparts to some of the more common Windows applications.

Ubuntu Linux is great for lots of reasons, but one of its strengths is the amount and type of applications the operating system ships with. If you are a new Ubuntu user, you're probably familiar with Windows and the application suites on that OS. Here's an introduction to the Ubuntu and open source analogues to those Windows-based applications you may use all the time. Feel free to play with these applications; they all have excellent help-based documentation if you get stuck.

Office Suite

One of the most commonly used Windows applications is Microsoft Office. Ubuntu ships with an office suite that's similar, called OpenOffice.org (sometimes called OOo). OpenOffice.org can even read and write Microsoft Office files, so you won't be left out of the loop when a friend or coworker emails you a document attachment. OpenOffice.org includes a word processor (Writer), shown in Figure 1-13; a spreadsheet (Calc); and a presentation tool (Impress). It also includes Math, a scientific formula editor; Draw, a flowchart and drawing program; and Base, a basic database. To access any of these programs, click on the Applications menu and select Office. All the OpenOffice.org applications are there. You can find out more about Open-Office.org from its web site (*http://www.openoffice.org*).

Graphics and Photo Editor

Adobe Photoshop is probably the most well-known photo and graphics editor. However, did you know that Ubuntu ships with a world-class graphics editor? This piece of software is called the GIMP (GNU Image Manipulation Program), and it's accessible from the Applications menu, in the graphics section. The GIMP (shown in Figure 1-14) includes many built-in filters for image manipulation and is scriptable using the programming language Python. It's so powerful, it's being used in some Hollywood studios! Surf over to the GIMP's web site (*http://www.gimp.org*) if you need more information.

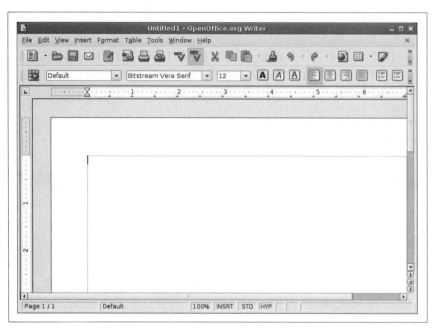

Figure 1-13. OpenOffice.Org Writer

Figure 1-14. The GIMP

Web Browsing

Web browsing in Ubuntu is handled by the super-popular Mozilla Firefox (*http://www.mozilla.org/firefox*) web browser (shown in Figure 1-15). Firefox comes in Windows and Macintosh versions, so you may have encountered it before. It has received much acclaim from the computer community in general—so much, in fact, that there's not much to add. To fire up Firefox, you can either click on the little world icon in the top panel, or you can run it via the Applications menu, in the Internet section.

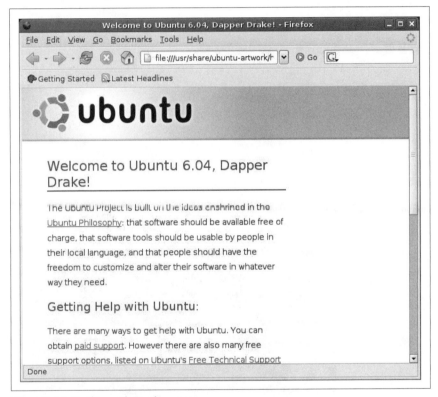

Figure 1-15. Surfing with Firefox

Email

The default mail program in Ubuntu is Evolution (*http://www.gnome.org/ projects/evolution/*). Evolution (shown in Figure 1-16) is much more than an email application, however. Like its counterpart, Microsoft Outlook,

Evolution is designed to manage contacts and calendars in addition to email. It even includes an integrated junk-mail function to help you deal with ever-increasing spam issues. You can launch Evolution by clicking on the little envelope icon in the top panel, or by going to the Internet section of the Applications menu.

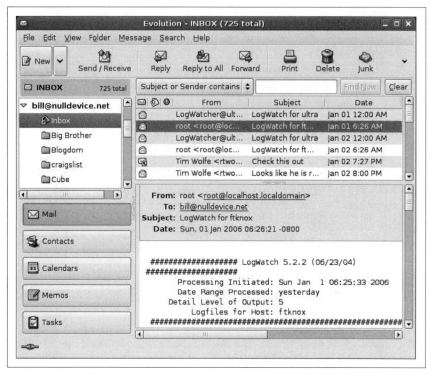

Figure 1-16. Reading mail with Evolution

Instant Messaging

Instant messaging has become a large part of the daily computing experience. Ubuntu's got you covered with the inclusion of Gaim (*http://gaim. sourceforge.net*), shown in Figure 1-17. Gaim is a cross-platform messaging client, able to communicate across the AOL, ICQ, MSN, Yahoo!, Google, and Jabber networks. It can even allow you to log in to multiple IM networks at the same time, thanks to its multiple-account support.

Figure 1-17. Messaging via Gaim

Media Player

Windows Media Player is the standard application for playing multimedia under Windows. Ubuntu ships with a similar program called Totem (*http://www.gnome.org/projects/totem/*), shown in Figure 1-18. Totem plays all manner of media, music, and video files. It supports playlists and streaming media as well, so you can use it to listen to Internet radio stations.

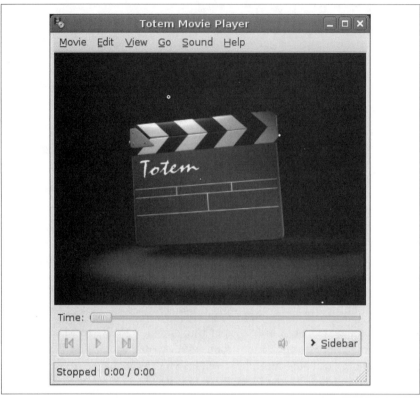

Figure 1-18. Using Totem for media

Whatever need you have, Ubuntu's probably got an application to fill it. If Ubuntu doesn't ship with it out of the box, it can probably be obtained via the Synaptic package manager or *apt-get*, thanks to the *universe* and *multiverse* repositories [Hack #60]. Have fun exploring the abilities of Ubuntu!

The Linux Desktop
Hacks 15–27

On its own, the X Window System (X11) isn't much of a friendly face. If you've ever run X11 without a window manager, you've no doubt seen it at its barest: a screen filled with a repeating crosshatch pattern, with an X for a mouse cursor. This simplicity does nothing to hint at X11's power, but once you've fired up GNOME, KDE, or any of the many window managers available for Ubuntu, you start to see what it's all about.

This chapter takes you a little deeper into the GNOME and KDE environments, which are so much more than window managers. You'll also learn how to check out some more lightweight window managers in case you're after something simpler and less CPU-intensive.

Once you're settled into your desktop environment, you're going to want to get some work done. This chapter shows you how to install Java, which is needed by many applications, including some of the peer-to-peer (P2P) applications discussed herein. You'll also learn how to connect your hand-held Palm or Pocket PC device to Ubuntu, work with remote file servers, and more.

HACK #15 Get Under the Hood of the GNOME Desktop

GNOME, the default Ubuntu desktop, is a powerful environment with a lot of features. Here is the information you need to quickly get up to speed on how to customize it.

Recently, the GNOME desktop seems to have lost some features. Looking around on mailing lists and reading people's blogs, you'll often find gripes about how some feature that was someone's personal favorite no longer exists. In reality, GNOME has far more features and configuration options available now than it ever had in the past—they're just hidden from sight, with users shown only the most commonly used options in the standard interface. This has the effect of making GNOME simpler and easier to use

for the average person, but it also makes it a prime target for getting under the hood and tweaking the deskop to suit your own tastes if you're an advanced user and want everything to work just the way you like it.

Configuration Nirvana: the Configuration Editor

GNOME provides a central mechanism called GConf for storing user preferences on behalf of individual applications. Instead of writing out their own preferences files and then parsing them again to read values back in, applications can simply use the GConf API. This has a number of benefits, such as the ability to share preference settings among applications and have preferences applied immediately to all running applications.

The GConf database is structured like a simple filesystem, containing keys organized into a tree hierarchy. Each key can be a directory that contains more keys, or it can have an actual value of its own. For example, the key */apps/nautilus/preferences* is a key that contains other keys (in a similar manner to a directory), and inside it is the */apps/nautilus/preferences/background_color* key with a default value of #ffffff. While keys are expressed as paths, as in a filesystem, they don't actually exist on disk in that way: they are stored in an XML document, with the path representing the nested items within it.

GConf has several tools that you can use to directly browse, query, and manipulate the database using either a GUI or the command line. Configuration Editor provides a very nice graphical interface to the database, but it doesn't appear in Ubuntu's Applications menu by default, so you can launch it from the command line:

```
$ gconf-editor
```

Alternatively, you can edit the Applications menu and add it. Go to Applications → Accessories → Alacarte Menu Editor, select System Tools, and turn on Configuration Editor, as shown in Figure 2-1.

Once you close the Menu Editor and return to the Applications menu, you'll find a new entry for Configuration Editor under System Tools.

When you open Configuration Editor, you'll notice that there is no Save button and all changes you make are applied immediately—so be careful! Browse around to see what options you can set for various applications, including Nautilus (the GNOME file manager) and Metacity (the default window manager). To get started, here are some specific options you can tweak with the *gconf-editor*:

Icons on desktop
    The default Ubuntu desktop configuration is totally empty: no trash can, no computer icon, no home icon. In Configuration Editor, go to

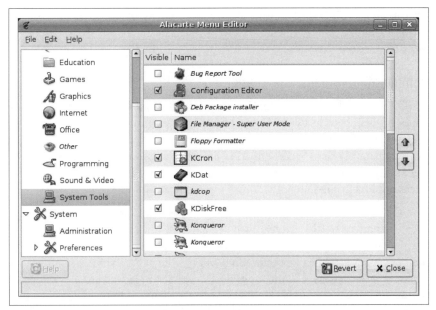

Figure 2-1. Edit the Applications menu

/apps/nautilus/desktop to see options to turn on or off a variety of desktop icons, as shown in Figure 2-2.

Empty trash without warnings

Emptying the trash generates an annoying confirmation message that has to be clicked, but you can suppress the confirmation by turning off */apps/nautilus/preferences/confirm_trash*.

And if you want to be able to bypass the Trash entirely and delete files by right-clicking on them, turn on *apps/nautilus/preferences/enable_delete* to add a "Delete" option to the right-click contextual menu. Now you can delete items immediately without sending them to the Trash first!

Open files with a single click

GNOME's default behavior is for a single-click to select files and a double-click to open them, but KDE and some other environments use a web-like "hot links" metaphor, in which files open on a single click. To enable the same behavior in GNOME, go to */apps/nautilus/preferences/click_policy* and replace the `double` value with `single`.

Scripting GConf

Automating changes to the GConf database is easy with tools such as *gconftool*, which is a command-line GConf client. Use it to read or set specific values in the database as well as explore its structure.

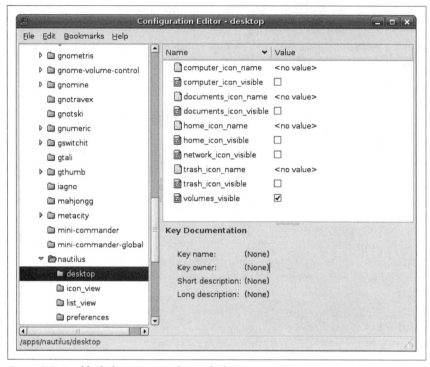

Figure 2-2. Enable desktop icons with gconf-editor

Recursively walk through parts of the database structure by specifying a starting point and using the -R (recursive read) option:

```
$ gconftool -R /apps/nautilus
```

Get the attribute type of a specific key using the -T (type) option:

```
$ gconftool -T /apps/nautilus/preferences/enable_delete
```

Read specific values by explicitly setting the key and using the -g (get) option:

```
$ gconftool -g /apps/nautilus/preferences/enable_delete
```

Write values by specifying the data type, using the -s (set) flag, the key, and the new value:

```
$ gconftool -t bool -s /apps/nautilus/preferences/enable_delete true
```

Writing values like this is a good way to demonstrate that changes really are immediate. Open up Configuration Editor and browse to */apps/nautilus/ preferences/*. Then watch the "enable_delete" checkbox while you set and unset the value using *gconftool*.

Once you get started, you'll find that your imagination is the limit when it comes to scripting GConf! For example, you could write a script that pulls down a webcam image every 10 minutes and then calls *gconftool* to set it as your desktop background. Make sure the image filename is different each time; otherwise, GConf won't see the change, and the background won't change:

```
$ gconftool -t string -s /desktop/gnome/background/picture_filename \
/home/jon/CamImages/Pic53332.jpg
```

Or you could set up a script to use XPlanet to generate an updated view of Earth and set it as your desktop background, and then call it from cron every 30 minutes. Install XPlanet:

```
$ sudo apt-get install xplanet xplanet-images
```

Then create a script to execute it. If you don't know the latitude and longitude of your city, you can probably find it (or a nearby city) in Wikipedia (*http://www.wikipedia.org*). Just adjust the following script to suit your location and screen resolution:

```
#!/bin/sh
rm -f /tmp/earth-*.jpg;
IMAGE=/tmp/earth-`date +%s`.jpg;
nice xplanet -num_times 1 -output $IMAGE -geometry 1280x1024 \
-longitude 96 -latitude 0;
gconftool -t string -s /desktop/gnome/background/picture_filename $IMAGE;
```

You can also use *gconftool* as a convenient way to add new URI handlers to GNOME. For example, to specify that you want *tel:* links to execute your Vonage client and initiate a call, you can run the following commands:

```
$ gconftool -t string -s /desktop/gnome/url-handlers/tel/command \
"bin/vonage-call %s"
$ gconftool -s /desktop/gnome/url-handlers/tel/needs_terminal false -t bool
$ gconftool -t bool -s /desktop/gnome/url-handlers/tel/enabled true
```

HACK #16 Tweak the KDE Desktop

Get up to speed with configuring KDE, the default desktop environment for the Kubuntu variant of Ubuntu.

While GNOME, the heart of Ubuntu, seems to be adopting an extremist policy of "simplify simplify simplify" that goes so far as to result in the father of Linux strongly criticizing it (see *http://mail.gnome.org/archives/usability/2005-December/msg00021.html*), KDE, the heart of Kubuntu, has sought to simplify without reducing features. Instead of simply hiding configuration options in the Windows Registry–like GConf or requiring that users know arcane key commands that serve to bring up important capabilities, both of which GNOME practices, KDE preserves the customizability and power

that has garnered it fans all over the world, while streamlining options and increasing ease of use.

A prime example of this can be seen in KDE's evolution from the Control Center to System Settings. The Control Center allowed users to customize KDE in virtually infinite ways, but its layout was cluttered and confusing, as shown in Figure 2-3.

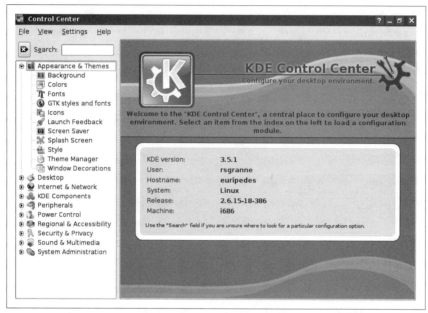

Figure 2-3. The old-fashioned KDE Control Center was pretty cluttered

The KDE developers responded to the criticisms they received and are transitioning to System Settings, which is found in Kubuntu (if, for some reason, it wasn't installed on your system, run the command sudo apt-get install kde-systemsettings to install it). As you can see in Figure 2-4, the layout is cleaner, easier to read, and more inviting. To start System Settings, click the K button and choose System Settings.

The infinite customizability is still present, but it's now more approachable for both experts and newbies. Instead of removing features or squirreling them away in byzantine ways, the KDE developers adopted an evolutionary path that improves usability without sacrificing power.

Right after I install Kubuntu, there are a few important changes I make using System Settings that I feel improve my use of KDE. Think of these as suggestions that you can try, but you really should explore the world of System Settings yourself to truly make your copy of Kubuntu your own.

Figure 2-4. The new and improved KDE System Settings

Personal

Click on the Panel button, and then on the Menus tab of Panels. Under QuickStart Menu Items, I like the fact that "Show the applications most frequently used" is selected, but in some cases, I've found that the number is set to 0. Change that to 5, and the five programs most frequently used in a session will show up at the top of the K menu, as you can see in Figure 2-5.

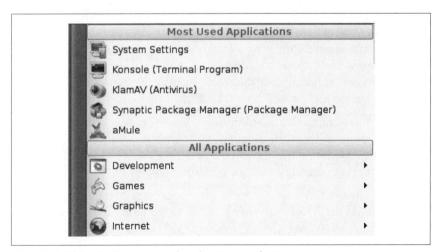

Figure 2-5. Show the five most used applications on the K menu

While also in Panel, select the Taskbar button. One of the so-called "innovations" that Windows XP introduced was *taskbar grouping*: if you have several windows from the same app open, they are grouped together as one button on the taskbar. To see the individual windows, select that taskbar button, holding down the mouse button, and a menu opens showing the various windows, which you can then pick from. Personally, I hate this feature. I want to see all open windows on a particular desktop, so I always change "Group similar tasks" from When Taskbar Full to Never. In addition, when I'm using multiple desktops, I don't want to see all the windows from all those desktops on the taskbar, which to me defeats the whole purpose of multiple desktops in the first place, so I uncheck "Show windows from all desktops" and "Sort windows by desktop." See Figure 2-6 for the changes I make.

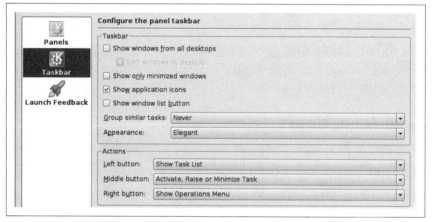

Figure 2-6. Turn off taskbar grouping

Back in System Settings, move on to Sound & Multimedia → System Notifications. I hate it when my computer constantly beeps and boops at me; the noise that KDE makes every time a window opens or closes drives me especially batty. I check the box for "Apply to all applications" and then click the Turn Off All button next to Sounds, shown in Figure 2-7.

Still, I like the sound KDE makes when it's first loading and when it's shutting down, so I always go ahead and click in the Sound column (the fifth column) next to "KDE is exiting" and "KDE is starting up," so I can hear those tiny melodies.

Hardware

In an effort to be more "web-like," the default behavior in KDE to open files and folders is a single click. While I love this behavior in Firefox, I don't like

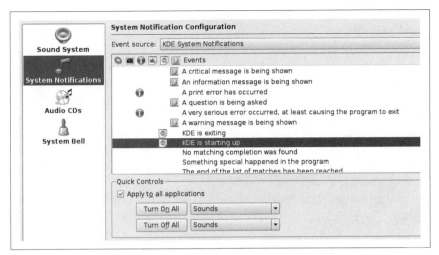

Figure 2-7. Turn off annoying system sounds

it so much in my file manager. To turn it off, select the Mouse button in the Hardware section and then, on the General tab, choose "Double-click to open files and folders."

System Administration

This one will help solve an annoyance that otherwise might cause U.S. users to smack their heads on their keyboards in frustration. In System Administration, choose "Regional and Accessibility," then "Country/Region and Language," and finally the "Other" tab. Change "Paper format" from A4 (which works great in Europe) to US Letter, the standard paper size in America. Now printing works again! And while you're there, change "Measure system" from Metric to Imperial, which is again what the U.S. uses. Of course, if your country's standards are different, here is where you change them.

When it comes to configuring KDE, I've just scratched the surface, but I hope this is enough to get you started. My advice is to click on every single item in System Settings and investigate what you find there. After you finish that, head over to *http://www.kde-look.org*, where you can download new wallpaper, themes, icons, styles, skins, screensavers, and splash screens to change how your copy of KDE appears. But KDE-Look.org isn't just about eye candy. You can also find service menus, software, improvements, and tips for changing how your KDE acts and behaves. It's a friendly, helpful community, and I know you'll find something fun and useful there. Linux is all about choice, and nowhere is that more obvious than when it comes to KDE and Kubuntu!

—Scott Granneman

Switch to a Lighter Window Manager

#17 GNOME and KDE are great, but they are a little heavy. If you're on an older system, or you just want a change of pace, you can use other window managers under Ubuntu, such as Fluxbox, XFCE, and Enlightenment.

If there's one thing that's great about Linux, it's choice. If you don't like a particular program, there's a pretty good chance that Linux has at least one alternative. This even applies to your entire desktop environment. The desktop environment comprises a lot of different programs, such as a window manager (which handles drawing borders around your windows, moving them, and so forth), panels so you can launch programs, background-management programs, and more. The most popular of these desktop environments are GNOME and KDE. Ubuntu defaults to GNOME [Hack #15] as its desktop environment but also offers a Kubuntu alternative [Hack #16] that automatically defaults to KDE instead.

If you don't particularly like GNOME or KDE, you still have other options. Linux has a large number of window managers that you can use instead of a full desktop environment such as GNOME or KDE, and all of the popular ones are available for Ubuntu. There are a number of reasons why you might want to give some of these window managers a try:

- Both GNOME and KDE need a fair amount of resources to run. Most of the alternative window managers require substantially fewer resources, so they might be attractive if you are using an older computer or if you just just want better performance out of your desktop.

- Alternative window managers often offer a totally different set of features and, in some cases, a different way to look at how to manage your windows. Some of these features include the ability to group windows into a single tabbed window (Fluxbox) or set up lots of fancy eye candy and control your windows' placement to a fine degree (Enlightenment).

If you want to stick with KDE or GNOME, there are some simple things you can do to lighten their resource usage. In KDE, run the program *kpersonalizer* (it's in the package of the same name) to reduce KDE's level of eye candy. In GNOME, use the Configuration Editor [Hack #15] to set */apps/metacity/general/reduced_resources* to true.

Even if you don't have a particular reason to try a different window manager, it doesn't hurt to install a few and see how they approach window management. You can easily switch back to your preferred desktop environment if you don't like them.

In this hack, we describe a few other window managers and how to install and use them in Ubuntu. There are hundreds of window managers we could cover, but here we will talk about three of the more popular alternatives to GNOME and KDE: XFCE, Fluxbox, and Enlightenment.

Generate Program Menus

The first step before you install a new window manager is to install and update a program to manage application menus so that you can launch applications without the GNOME or KDE launchers. Use your preferred package installation tool and install the package called *menu*. Once the program is installed, open a terminal and update the current list of programs for this menu:

```
$ sudo update-menus
```

Change to Your New Window Manager

We will discuss how to install and use each of the different window managers, but since you will use the same method to change to each of them, we'll describe that first. Each of these window managers is integrated with the desktop manager Ubuntu uses (GDM by default, KDM for Kubuntu) and will add itself to the list of available sessions when you install it.

After you install a particular window manager, log out of your current desktop environment to get to the main login screen. Click on the Sessions button to see a list of available desktop environments and window managers, and select the window manager you'd like to try. After you log in, you will be presented with the option to accept this window manager permanently or to accept it just for this session. If you want to switch back, log out and then select your previous window manager from the list (GNOME under Ubuntu, KDE under Kubuntu).

Try XFCE

If you are interested in other window managers or desktop environments, probably one of the first desktop environments to try is XFCE. XFCE (*http:// www.xfce.org*) aims to be lightweight, so you will get many of the familiar features of a full desktop environment—such as a panel, desktop icons, and a taskbar—but with improved performance.

To install XFCE, use your preferred package-installation program to install the *xfce4* package. The desktop environment and many accompanying tools will be installed. XFCE has a number of other nonessential plug-ins and

programs that you can install as well. Just use your package manager's search tool with the keyword xfce to show them all.

Once XFCE is installed, log out, choose the XFCE session, log in, and you will be presented with the default XFCE desktop (see Figure 2-8).

Figure 2-8. The default Ubuntu XFCE desktop

XFCE is organized into a panel at the bottom where you can launch common tools such as a terminal, XFCE's file manager *xffm*, a web browser, and other applications. To launch applications that aren't in the panel, right-click on the desktop to open the main menu. You can change a launcher's settings by right-clicking on it in the panel. You can also right-click on other parts of the panel to add new items, such as launchers, pagers, and other programs.

Along the top of the desktop is the taskbar, where you can see and switch between all open applications on the current desktop. Right-click on one of the applications in the taskbar to get extra options, such as the ability to maximize, close, and hide the program.

XFCE provides a graphical configuration tool you can access by clicking on the wrench icon in the panel. This program lets you configure anything from the desktop background to keybindings, screensaver settings, and the taskbar.

Click the User Interface icon to open the theme manager, where you can configure the look and feel of XFCE.

To log out of XFCE, click the power icon on the panel, or right-click on the desktop and choose Quit. For more information about XFCE, visit the official page at *http://www.xfce.org*.

Use Fluxbox

Fluxbox (*http://www.fluxbox.org*) is an alternative window manager that is popular for its speed and ability to group windows into tabs. While it is relatively lightweight, Fluxbox offers a number of features, including the ability to remember window placement, configurable panels, and add-ons that let you have icons on your desktop (*fbdesk*) and a pager (*fbpager*).

To install Fluxbox, select the *fluxbox* package in your preferred package management tool. After it is installed, log out of your current desktop environment, select the Fluxbox session, and log back in to see the default Fluxbox desktop, shown in Figure 2-9.

Figure 2-9. Default Ubuntu Fluxbox desktop

By default, the Fluxbox desktop is pretty bare; there is only a small panel along the bottom of the screen. This panel contains a taskbar to display all applications open on the current desktop and can switch to new desktops. Right-click on the panel to change panel-specific options.

Instead of an application menu in the panel, Fluxbox displays the menu whenever you right-click on the desktop. In addition to the standard application categories, such as Apps and Games, the main menu has a Configuration submenu where you can configure Fluxbox settings—including how it focuses windows and toolbar settings, as shown in Figure 2-10. There is also a Styles menu that lets you change the theme.

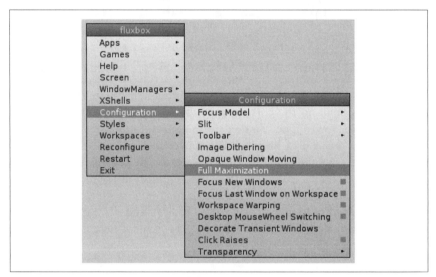

Figure 2-10. Fluxbox Configuration submenu

As mentioned previously, Fluxbox allows you to group windows together with tabs. Middle-click on the titlebar of a window and then drag and drop it onto another window. Fluxbox will automatically tab the windows together so that you can click on one of the tabs on the titlebar to select a window. To remove a tab, middle-click on it in the titlebar and drag and drop it onto the desktop.

To exit Fluxbox, right-click on the desktop and select Exit. For more information on Fluxbox, visit the main project page at *http://www.fluxbox.org*.

Seek Enlightenment

Enlightenment (*http://www.enlightenment.org*) has long been known as the window manager with all the eye candy. Back in the days of 100 MHz processors, it was also known as being slow. These days, Enlightenment offers the same eye candy with almost infinite configurability and, with modern computers, a really snappy response.

To install Enlightenment, install the *enlightenment* package with your preferred package manager. In addition, you may want to install the *e16keyedit*

and *e16menuedit* tools, since they provide the GUI to edit your keybindings and main menu, respectively. After the *enlightenment* package is installed, log out of your current desktop, choose the Enlightenment session, and then log back in.

The default Enlightenment desktop is almost as bare as Fluxbox (see Figure 2-11). Along the top is a desktop dragbar, which you can use to switch desktops. If you are on any desktop other than the main root desktop, you can also drag the desktop dragbar down to reveal the desktop underneath. At the bottom left of the desktop is the Enlightenment pager. The pager displays a view of each desktop, along with any windows open on that desktop. You can drag and drop windows from one desktop to another by dragging them within the pager, or even by dragging them from the pager and dropping them on the current desktop. Along the bottom right of the desktop is the *iconbox*. The iconbox stores icons for any windows you *iconify* (minimize), instead of having them appear in a taskbar. Right-click on the iconbox to configure its settings, including its size and whether the background is transparent. To access the main application menu, middle-click on the desktop. Right-click on the desktop to configure Enlightenment settings, including the number of desktops, background settings, and so on. Right-click and select Special FX Settings to see the different types of eye candy you can configure.

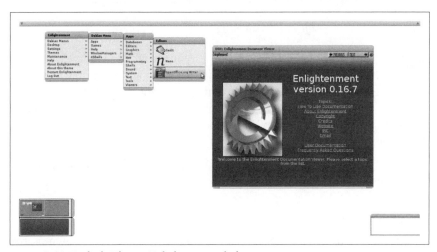

Figure 2-11. Default Ubuntu Enlightenment desktop

Enlightenment also offers *advanced window memory*. Window memory allows you to remember settings about a particular window, such as its location, its size, which desktop it's on, and other settings. The next time you start the program, Enlightenment will remember and use any or all of the

settings you told it to remember. This way, you can, for instance, always have your web browser open on a particular desktop. To configure which settings to remember, right-click on the titlebar for a window and select Remember.

Window grouping is another feature Enlightenment offers that many other window managers don't. To group windows, right-click the titlebar on the first window and select Window Groups → "Start a new group." Then right-click on the titlebar for any other windows you want to group with it and select Window Groups → "Add this Window to the Current Group." When windows are grouped, they can all be configured to mimic operations performed on any other window in the group. For instance, if you minimize one window in the group, the rest will minimize. If you move one window, the others will move along with it. To configure which behaviors all members of a group will adhere to, right-click on the titlebar for one of the windows and select Window Groups → "Configure this Window's Groups."

To exit Enlightenment, middle-click on the desktop and select Log Out. For more information about Enlightenment, middle-click on the desktop and select Help, or you can visit the main project page at *http://www.enlightenment.org*.

Other Window Managers

There are plenty of other window managers you can install under Ubuntu, such as Blackbox, Openbox, WindowMaker, Afterstep, and FVWM. To install any of these window managers, search for its name in your preferred package manager and then install the corresponding package. Most of the major window managers will add themselves to your sessions menu so you can easily select them when you log in.

Install Java

The modern web-browsing experience requires Java. Here's how to install Java and caffeinate your web browser.

Ubuntu's an amazing Linux distribution for lots of different reasons, but one of the things people find attractive about it is the fact that it ships with lots of different software, preconfigured and ready to use. However, until recently, one of the things that the Ubuntu developers couldn't include was the Sun Java Runtime Environment (JRE), because it used a nonfree license that prevented its bundling with a Linux distribution.

Recently, however, Sun Microsystems relaxed the restrictions on the Java license, introducing the Distro License for Java (DLJ). This new license allows distributors to ship Sun's JRE and Java Development Kit (JDK) as installable

packages, rather than the self-extracting binaries that were previously available. It also gives Linux distributors the ability to define the packaging, installation, and support for Java within their Linux distribution.

As such, Dapper Drake now ships with Sun's Java available as a non-free package in the *multiverse* repository. You'll need to have the *universe* and *multiverse* repositories enabled [Hack #60] to install Java.

The Ubuntu developers have separated the Java components into several packages:

sun-java5-bin
> Contains the binaries

sun-java5-demo
> Contains demos and examples

sun-java5-doc
> Contains the documentation

sun-java5-fonts
> Contains the Lucida TrueType fonts from the JRE

sun-java5-jdk
> Contains the metapackage for the JDK

sun-java5-jre
> Contains the metapackage for the JRE

sun-java5-plugin
> Contains the plug-in for Mozilla-based browsers

sun-java5-source
> Contains source files for the JDK

Installing the Java Runtime Environment

Once you've got the *multiverse* repository enabled, installing Sun's Java package is easy. Simply open a terminal window and *apt-get* the package. Since you are going to be installing the JRE and the web browser plug-in, you'll be using the following command from a terminal window:

```
bill@constellation:~$ sudo apt-get install sun-java5-jre sun-java5-plugin \
                      sun-java5-fonts
```

Once *apt-get* downloads the packages and begins the installation, you'll get a screen that contains the Sun Operating System Distributor License for Java. Read the license, if you wish, and hit Enter to continue. You'll see a dialog that asks you if you agree with the DLJ license terms. Select Yes, and hit Enter; the JRE will finish installing.

At this point, Java is installed.

Confirming the Installation

You'll want to confirm that your system is configured properly for Sun's JRE. This is a two-step process. First, check that the JRE is properly installed by running the following command from a terminal. You should get similar output:

```
bill@constellation:~$ java -version
java version "1.5.0_06"
Java(TM) 2 Runtime Environment, Standard Edition (build 1.5.0_06-b05)
Java HotSpot(TM) Client VM (build 1.5.0_06-b05, mixed mode, sharing)
```

 If you see an unexpected version of Java—in particular, one identified as "gij (GNU libgcj)"—then you probably have GNU Java installed. You can easily switch from one Java to another with the command sudo update-alternatives --config java, which will prompt you to choose which Java implementation to use. Pick the one in */usr/lib/jvm* to use the JRE you just installed.

If the JRE is properly installed, confirm that the Java plug-in is installed in your browser by opening Firefox and typing about:plugins in the address bar (see Figure 2-12).

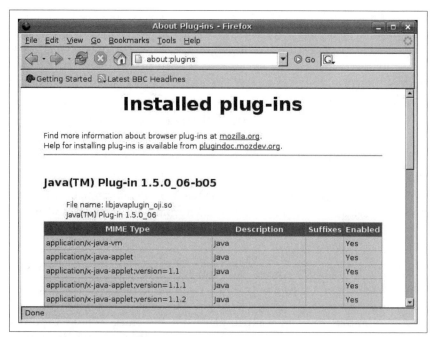

Figure 2-12. Verifying that the Java web plug-in is installed

Congratulations, you've caffeinated your browser! You can now surf to Java-enabled web sites and use Java applications!

HACK #19 Search Your Computer

Have Beagle find and fetch your information faster than you thought possible.

One of Linux's weaker points as a desktop OS has been the lack of a search feature. Nautilus has had a "find this file" function for quite some time, but it's really not much more sophisticated than a GUI wrapper around the command-line *find* command. Both Nautilus and the *find* command do similar things: they'll look at each and every file in the directory structure, trying to find a match for the criteria you've given them.

There is a better way to search a filesystem. It involves creating an index of all the files on that filesystem, which enables you to search the index much like you would a database. This is what Windows and Mac OS X do for their file-search capabilities, and now Linux has it too in the form of Beagle, a modular search engine that's written in Mono. It's easy to add Beagle to Ubuntu, and the usability benefits are tremendous.

Installing Beagle

In this hack, you'll be installing Beagle and a very cool search frontend known as *deskbar-applet*. *deskbar-applet* sits in your GNOME panel and enables all manner of search goodness for you. As with many optional goodies, you'll need to have the *universe* repository enabled [Hack #60] to install both of these packages. Now, open up a terminal [Hack #13] and install *beagle* and *deskbar-applet*:

```
bill@lexington:~$ sudo aptitude install beagle deskbar-applet
```

Starting beagled

Once you've got *beagle* and *deskbar-applet* installed, you'll need to start *beagled* (the main engine and database) manually. From a terminal, you'll simply run *beagled*. It should start and detach from your terminal, and run in the background:

```
bill@lexington:~$ beagled
```

It will then begin the process of indexing your hard disk(s). This will take a while, depending on the amount and type of data you have. We have seen *beagled* take up to three hours to fully index a disk. If you're running *beagled* on a laptop, you may want to make sure it's plugged into AC power, because the high I/O from *beagled*'s initial indexing could drain your

battery. While *beagled* is indexing, you can set up your GNOME desktop to automatically start *beagled* when you log in. Simply click on the System Menu, and select Preferences and then Sessions. Add *beagled* to your Startup Programs, and it will be ready to fetch stuff for you on your next login.

Using Beagle and deskbar-applet

Now that the Beagle daemon is running, it's time to add *deskbar-applet* to the mix. The deskbar applet is a GNOME applet, so add it to one of the GNOME panels by right-clicking on the panel and selecting "Add to Panel." Select Deskbar, click Add, and then close the window. You'll see the deskbar in your panel now.

At this point, you can put criteria into the deskbar applet and go ahead and search for something (see Figure 2-13). If you put your search criteria in the applet and click the little magnifying glass, you can tell the deskbar applet to search any one of a number of databases, including Beagle, which is not enabled by default. (The default search can be changed in the preferences for *deskbar-applet*; simply right-click on the applet and select Preferences to adjust it.)

Figure 2-13. Searching Beagle with deskbar

Once you click on "Search for...using Beagle," Beagle takes over, digging through its index and fetching the proper results. By default, Beagle will search the files in your home directory, as well as metadata like email archives, instant messages, and blog posts. It doesn't matter where the data is; Beagle will fetch it for you (see Figure 2-14).

Figure 2-14. Beagle fetching data

As you start to use Beagle, you'll gradually see the benefit of having an agent index all your data and metadata. It may sound clichéd, but over time, this will change the way you work.

HACK #20   Access Remote Filesystems

Use integrated desktop tools to access a number of different remote network shares.

Let's face it: sometimes it's difficult to fit all of the files you need on a single computer. Whether they be Windows shares at your office, FTP servers somewhere on the Internet, or even machines on the network running SSH,

you can access all of these servers and more from the Ubuntu desktop with a few clicks.

The key to connecting to remote filesystems is the "Connect to Server" dialog window. Click Places → Connect to Server to see the default window, shown in Figure 2-15.

Connect to Server	✕
Service type:	Public FTP
Server:	
Optional information:	
Port:	
Folder:	
Name to use for connection:	
Browse Network	✕ Cancel	Connect

Figure 2-15. A sample "Connect to Server" dialog for FTP connections

There are a number of different connection types the dialog supports. Figure 2-16 shows the options available from the drop-down menu. Apart from a few specific options, each of these connection types shares the same sorts of options. The top of the window requests the location of the server (a hostname or IP address), and then below that is a list of nonessential options you can configure. For instance, you can give each of your connections custom names so that they are easier to tell apart from each other.

Connecting to a Windows share is a good example of how to use the "Connect to Server" dialog. First, select "Windows share" from the drop-down menu. Then, fill in the name of the server you want to connect to and, optionally, the name of the share you want to connect to (Figure 2-17). If your network requires authentication, you can also configure the username and domain name in this window. Once you have configured the share, click the Connect button. A new icon for this share will then appear on your desktop. Double-click that icon to open the Nautilus file browser to that share.

If you aren't quite sure about the settings for your Windows share, you can also click Browse Network to search the local network for any available Windows shares.

Figure 2-16. The submenu shows the different types of remote servers you can connect to

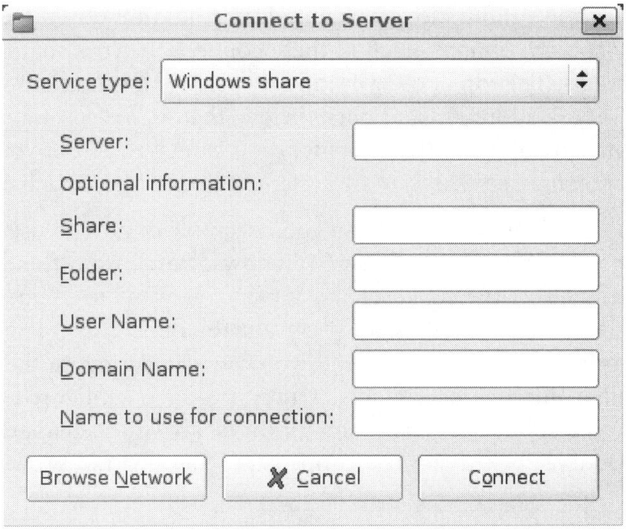

Figure 2-17. Sample "Windows share" dialog without any fields filled in

One of the more interesting abilities of the "Connect to Server" dialog is to connect to remote SSH servers and share files over SFTP. Not only does this mean that you don't have to configure any special file sharing on the remote machine, but any machine that runs SSH is now also a file share you can access. What's more, all of the communication is sent over an encrypted channel.

To connect to a remote SSH server, select SSH from the "Service type" drop-down menu. In Figure 2-18, you can see a sample window filled out with information to connect to a server on the network. By default, the SSH connection will open into the / directory, but you can change that to any directory you wish in the Folder field. If you needed to connect to the remote server as a different user, you could also specify that in this window. Finally, you can give this share a custom name that will appear both on its icon in the desktop and in the sidebar of the file browser.

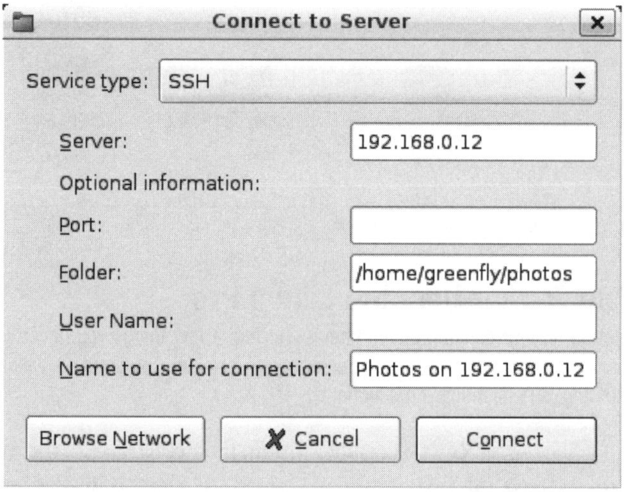

Figure 2-18. You can even connect to remote servers securely over SSH

Once you click Connect, a new icon appears on the desktop, and if you double-click it, you can access all of the photos on the remote server, as shown in Figure 2-19. You can then drag and drop them to and from the local machine as you do with any other directory.

If you decide that you no longer want to access a particular share, just right-click on its icon on the desktop and select Unmount Volume. Otherwise, file shares will appear both in the sidebar of your file manager and in the Places → Network Servers window.

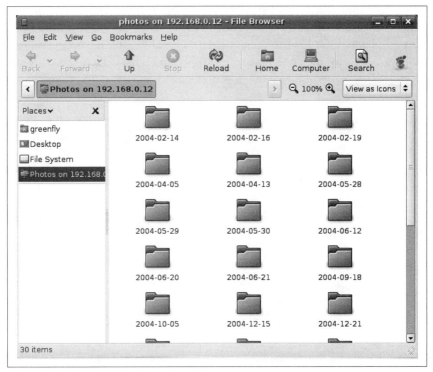

Figure 2-19. Some files accessed over SSH

Tweak Your Desktop Like a Pro

Customize your desktop environment, and find a few things you never knew you needed, like a pop-up Quake-style terminal, automatic wallpaper shuffling, and dashboard functionality.

The default Ubuntu GNOME environment is very streamlined and easy to use. Due to its ease of use, however, some of the "power user" features aren't included in the base install. KDE can also benefit from the same tweaking. Here's how to get more usability and features from Ubuntu.

Get Icons on Your Desktop

The default Ubuntu Dapper Drake desktop has no icons on it—which gives the system a very clean and simple look. If you're coming from Windows, you may miss the My Computer icon and other desktop icons in that OS. It's relatively simple to add them to Ubuntu; it just requires the use of a configuration editor called *gconf-editor* [Hack #15].

If you hit Alt-F2, the system will pop up a Run Application dialog. Type gconf-editor in that dialog and click Run. The Gconf configuration program

will start. Select "apps" from the left pane; then select "nautilus" and "desktop." In the right pane, you will see several options, like "computer_icon_name" and "computer_icon_visible." If you click on the checkbox next to the "<name>_icon_visible" option (see Figure 2-20), Nautilus will spontaneously add that icon to your desktop. In this fashion, you can add icons for your computer, home directory, network places, documents, and wastebasket.

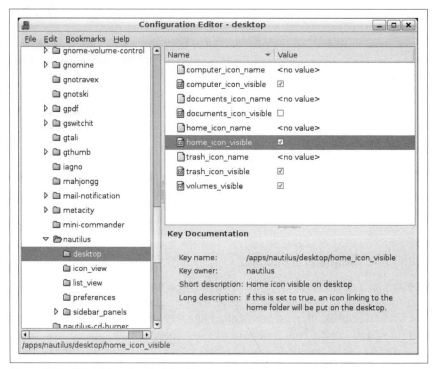

Figure 2-20. GConf showing the Nautilus icon-configuration options

Get Organized with Tomboy

Tomboy, shown in Figure 2-21, is a tiny application that sits in your panel and acts as an always-on mini Wiki. It's great for making quick notes to yourself without worrying about saving myriad text files or waiting for an editor to start. Much like a Wiki, you can cross-reference the Tomboy notes you make using Wiki-like annotations. Not only that, but the notes are quickly searchable using Tomboy's built-in search capabilities.

To install Tomboy, just *apt-get* it from a terminal:

```
bill@defiant:~$ sudo apt-get install tomboy
```

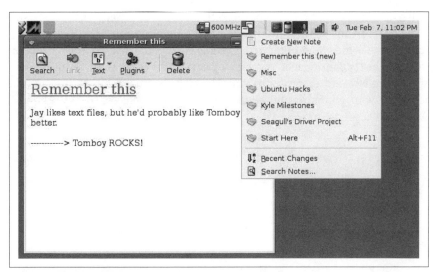

Figure 2-21. Tomboy notes

That will fetch and install Tomboy and its dependencies. Once that's completed, you can add Tomboy to your panel by right-clicking on the panel, selecting "Add to Panel," and then choosing Tomboy Notes from the dialog.

Automatic Wallpaper Switching

Something GNOME doesn't provide for is a way to automatically rotate your desktop wallpaper. Luckily, there's a little application written by someone known only as "Earthworm" called *wp_tray* that will sit in your notification area and rotate your wallpaper based on whatever scheme you wish. The source code for this application is at *http://planetearthworm.com/projects/wp_tray/files/wp_tray-0.4.6.tar.gz*, but Bill has built it for Ubuntu and made it available at *http://wildbill.nulldevice.net/ubuntu/wp-tray_0.4.6-1_i386.deb*. Download the *.deb* for *wp_tray* and install it using the following command:

```
bill@defiant:~$ sudo dpkg -i wp-tray_0.4.6-1_i386.deb
```

Once *wp_tray* is installed, add it to your startup programs so it starts when you log in: click on the System Menu, then Preferences, then Sessions, and add *wp_tray* to the list of Startup Programs. Log out and log in again, and you will be able to right-click on the applet (see Figure 2-22) and configure it to your wishes (Figure 2-23).

Figure 2-22. The interface to wp_tray

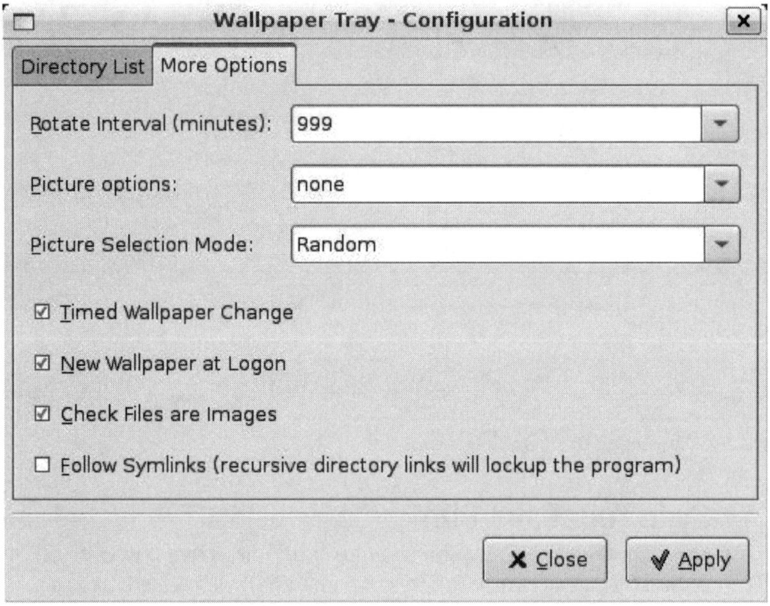

Figure 2-23. wp_tray's configuration screen

Getting a Pull-Down "Quake" Terminal

There's a very useful KDE application called *yakuake* that takes the standard KDE Konsole and changes it to a drop-down, on-demand terminal over your desktop and applications. (It's called a "Quake" terminal because of its resemblence to the console that drops down in the Quake series of games.) This is a very handy little application. To install, simply use *apt-get* to install both *konsole* and *yakuake*:

```
bill@lexington:~$ sudo apt-get install konsole yakuake
```

Add *yakuake* to your startup session using the same instructions for the *wp_ tray* applet. Log out and log in again, and then you can hit F12 to cause *yakuake* to drop down over your desktop, as shown in Figure 2-24.

Figure 2-24. yakuake: the drop-down konsole

Sync Your Palm PDA

HACK #22

Your Palm OS handheld can join in on the Ubuntu fun. Learn how to install applications on your Palm or Treo, keep it in sync with Evolution, and back it up.

Getting a Palm OS PDA to synchronize with Linux has usually involved some amount of effort, and some pain installing and configuring the necessary software. The folks working on Ubuntu have made it easy, however. Ubuntu includes all the software necessary to synchronize your Palm with Evolution and do almost everything you've done under Windows.

Configuring Palm Synchronization

Since the Ubuntu and Evolution developers included the *gnome-pilot* package in Ubuntu, there's no software that needs to be installed. Everything you need is on your system; it just needs to be configured to sync with your Palm.

To begin the configuration process, start Evolution, click on the Edit menu, and select Synchronization Options. The *gnome-pilot* splash screen will appear (see Figure 2-25). Click on Forward to proceed.

Figure 2-25. The gnome-pilot startup dialog

Next, *gnome-pilot* displays the Cradle Settings dialog, shown in Figure 2-26. Put values corresponding to your Palm and your system in this dialog box. For instance, USB-equipped Palms will probably sync using port */dev/ttyUSB0* and a speed of 115200, and they will require the USB radio button to be selected. Older, serial Palms will probably need the port set to */dev/ttyS0* and a speed of 57600, and they will need the Serial radio button selected. Click on Forward to continue.

Now it's time to identify the Palm (see Figure 2-27). If you've synchronized your Palm with another PC or operating system before, select "Yes, I've used sync software with this pilot before." If you have never synchronized your Palm, select "No, I've never used sync software with this pilot before." If you select No, ensure that your User Name is set to something you'd like the Palm to have embedded in it. The ID string doesn't require any changes or editing. Click on Forward to move to the next step (initial sync).

At this point, you'll be prompted to press the Hotsync button on your Palm. Press it, and you should hear a couple of quick beeps from the Palm. Click Forward to move on to the next step.

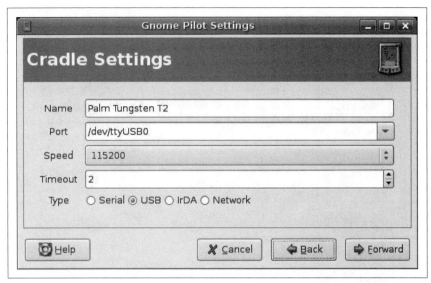

Figure 2-26. The Cradle Settings dialog

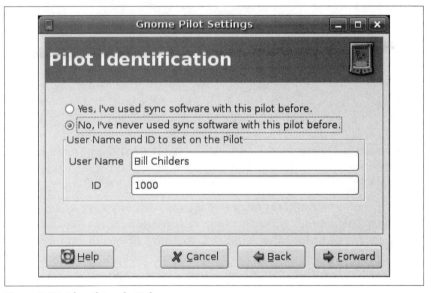

Figure 2-27. Identifying the Palm

The next screen (see Figure 2-28) asks you to enter a descriptive name for your Palm and a directory path. It defaults to MyPilot; you can leave it at the default or change it as we have.

You're now done configuring the Palm sync method. Click on the Apply button (see Figure 2-29) to commit the configuration.

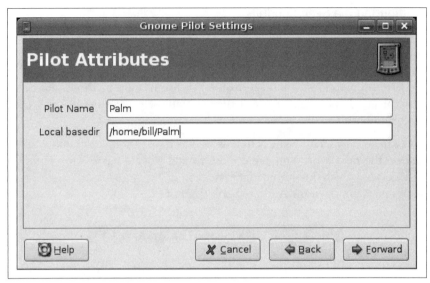

Figure 2-28. Setting the Pilot attributes

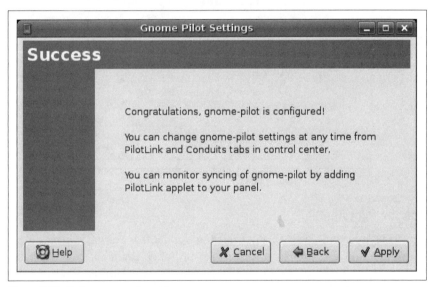

Figure 2-29. Palm sync configured

   Your sync may not initiate automatically. You may have to
mount the *usbfs* by entering sudo mount -t usbfs none /proc/
bus/usb/ at a terminal window. This is to work around a
change the Dapper developers made.

Configuring the Sync Conduits

The only thing that remains is to configure the individual synchronization conduits. In Evolution, go back to the Edit menu and select Synchronization Options. The Pilot Settings dialog is where you can enable and disable the Evolution conduits, and set up the synchronization methods and rules. To edit conduits, click on the Conduits tab, select a conduit, and click Enable or Disable.

You can set the default sync action as well as a one-time action that will fire just on the next sync. You can choose to add private records to your sync and decide which Evolution database you'd like to sync to. Figure 2-30 shows an example of the Address Book conduit.

Figure 2-30. Address Book sync options

Add the Pilot Applet

To make sure the GNOME Pilot daemon (*gpilotd*) is started when you log in, you should add the Pilot Applet to your panel. Right-click on the panel and choose Add To Panel. Locate Pilot Applet under Utilities, and add this to the panel. You can click the applet to bring up the conduit settings and right-click it to get a menu with several options, shown in Figure 2-31.

At this point, your Palm is ready to sync with Evolution. Simply hook up the Palm and initiate a hotsync, and it'll sync with Linux just like it did under Windows.

Figure 2-31. Pilot Applet option menu

Sync Your Pocket PC

Just because your Pocket PC is powered by Windows doesn't mean you can't sync it with Ubuntu.

Inside the box of your Pocket PC, you'll find a USB cable that's compatible with nearly every computer on the planet. What you won't find is software that's compatible with anything other than Windows. To sync your Pocket PC with Ubuntu, you'll need some additional software. Fortunately, most of this software is available in Ubuntu's *universe* repository.

ActiveSync, the software that comes with your Pocket PC, takes care of synchronizing calendars and contacts, and also installing applications in the Pocket PC. With the *ipaq* USB-serial module, the SynCE suite of tools, and Multisync, you can do all of this on your Linux system.

Connecting the Pocket PC

The first order of business is to figure out which interface your Pocket PC uses. If you're using a recent Pocket PC, it will probably look like an iPAQ as far as Linux is concerned. Before you plug in your Pocket PC, run sudo modprobe ipaq to load the iPAQ USB-to-serial driver. Plug in your Pocket PC and examine the output of *dmesg* to see whether it was detected and which device represents it. In the following example, a Pocket PC was detected on */dev/ttyUSB0*:

```
bjepson@ubuntu:~$ sudo modprobe ipaq
Password:
bjepson@ubuntu:~$ dmesg | tail
```

```
[ 1720.274390] usbcore: registered new driver usbserial
[ 1720.285461] drivers/usb/serial/usb-serial.c: USB Serial support
registered for generic
[ 1720.317318] usbcore: registered new driver usbserial_generic
[ 1720.319073] drivers/usb/serial/usb-serial.c: USB Serial Driver core
[ 1720.415421] drivers/usb/serial/usb-serial.c: USB Serial support
registered for PocketPC PDA
[ 1720.448394] drivers/usb/serial/ipaq.c: USB PocketPC PDA driver v0.5
[ 1720.457095] usbcore: registered new driver ipaq
[ 1738.233238] usb 1-1: new full speed USB device using ohci_hcd and address
2
[ 1738.796279] ipaq 1-1:1.0: PocketPC PDA converter detected
[ 1738.803167] usb 1-1: PocketPC PDA converter now attached to ttyUSB0
```

> Unfortunately, this probably won't work with a Pocket PC
> that's too new. At the time of this writing, SynCE did not yet
> support the most recent Pocket PC operating system, Win-
> dows Mobile 5.0.

The next thing you'll need to do is install some packages, but before you do
so, make sure you've enabled the *universe* repository in */etc/apt/sources.list*.
Then, run sudo apt-get update to get the latest packages and install *synce*,
dccm, and some supporting tools:

```
bjepson@ubuntu:~$ sudo apt-get install synce-dccm synce-serial librra0-tools
```

When *dpkg* hits the *synce-serial* package, it will ask you for a few things: the
serial interface used by your Pocket PC, the IP addresses for the PPP connection used with your Pocket PC, and the IP address of your DNS server. You
need to provide the DNS server address, but you can accept the defaults for
the rest (although you should check the serial interface against what you
found earlier in the output of *dmesg*). Although you specified the serial port
during the setup, I've found that you need to do it once more after installation, so run this command:

```
bjepson@ubuntu:~$ sudo synce-serial-config /dev/ttyUSB0
```

You can now run synce-serial-start to start a serial connection.

Testing the Connection

Now it's time to give it a try. Make sure your Pocket PC is connected to your
computer, and start the *dccm* daemon. Without arguments, it will run in the
background. Since this is its first time out, I suggest starting it in the fore-
ground (-f) with debugging enabled (-d 4):

```
bjepson@ubuntu:~$ dccm -d 4 -f
dccm[4599]: Running in foreground
dccm[4599]: Listening for connections on port 5679
```

Open another terminal and start up SynCE:

```
bjepson@ubuntoo2:~$ sudo synce-serial-start

synce-serial-start is now waiting for your device to connect
```

If you see the error "synce-serial-abort was unable find a running SynCE connection. Will do nothing," then the Pocket PC has probably gone to sleep while you were setting things up. If it did, it will disconnect from the machine, and */dev/ttyUSB0* will disappear. If you see "PocketPC PDA converter now disconnected from ttyUSB0" in the output of *dmesg*, unplug it and plug it back in, and try *synce-serial-start* again.

Once you have the connection up and running, the Pocket PC should stay awake.

Watch the shell where you started *dccm* and wait a while; it can take anywhere from 30 seconds to a minute for the Pocket PC and *dccm* to start chatting. Once they begin talking to one another, you'll see something like this:

```
dccm[4941]: Connection from 192.168.131.201 accepted
info package (104 bytes):
  0000: 28 00 00 00 04 14 00 00  (.......
  0008: 11 0a 00 00 00 00 00 00  ........
  0010: 2a 1e c3 37 00 00 00 00  *..7....
  0018: 28 00 00 00 3c 00 00 00  (....
  0020: 5a 00 00 00 00 00 00 00  Z.......
  0028: 50 00 6f 00 63 00 6b 00  P.o.c.k.
  0030: 65 00 74 00 5f 00 50 00  e.t._.P.
  0038: 43 00 00 00 50 00 6f 00  C...P.o.
  0040: 63 00 6b 00 65 00 74 00  c.k.e.t.
  0048: 50 00 43 00 00 00 53 00  P.C...S.
  0050: 53 00 44 00 4b 00 00 00  S.D.K...
  0058: 00 00 50 00 57 00 31 00  ..P.W.1.
  0060: 30 00 42 00 31 00 00 00  0.B.1...
  0068:
dccm[4941]: Talking to 'Pocket_PC', a PocketPC device of type PW10B1
```

To disconnect the Pocket PC, first run the command killall -HUP dccm. If all went well, you should see "Connection interrupted" and "Connection from 192.168.131.201 closed" in the *dccm* session. You can leave *dccm* running. To reconnect, run sudo synce-serial-start again.

Establish a Partnership

Before you can sync to the Pocket PC, you'll need to set up a partnership. Pocket PCs can be partnered with at most two computers, so if you've already configured your Pocket PC with a Windows computer running

ActiveSync, you'll have one slot left. The *synce-matchmaker* program will pick an empty slot and use it:

```
bjepson@ubuntoo2:~$ synce-matchmaker create
[rra_matchmaker_create_partnership:356] Partnership slot 1 is empty on
device
[rra_matchmaker_create_partnership:356] Partnership slot 2 is empty on
device
Partnership creation succeeded. Using partnership index 1.
```

If you don't have a free slot, you'll need to pick one to remove. See the *synce-matchmaker* manpage for details.

> You need to run *synce-matchmaker* only once to pair it with your computer.

Synchronize with Evolution

To synchronize your Pocket PC with Evolution, you'll need to install Multisync (*http://multisync.sourceforge.net*), a modular synchronization package that lets you create pairs of repositories that are kept in sync. To install Multisync and the SynCE plug-in, issue the command sudo apt-get install libmultisync-plugin-all synce-multisync-plugin, which will also install a collection of plug-ins, including the Evolution plug-in and the backup plug-in. You'll use the backup plug-in to verify that Multisync is running correctly before you try to synchronize it with SynCE.

> At the time of this writing, most of the pieces required to sync a Pocket PC with KDE were present in Ubuntu, but they did not work well together. In particular, the Raki panel applet would segfault when it tried to set up a partnership, and the *syncekonnector*, required for syncing PIM information with KDE, did not build against the versions of various libraries included with Dapper. However, for those inclined to compile a handful of libraries from scratch, there is a HOWTO for Debian users at *http://sourceforge.net/mailarchive/forum. php?thread_id=9562091&forum_id=15200*.

Don't look for Multisync in Evolution: you won't find it under Edit → Synchronization Options or Edit → Plugins. You'll need to launch the *multisync* application under X11 to work with it (you can either launch it from a shell or load it from Applications → Accessories → Multisync). When you launch Multisync, its main window appears, as shown in Figure 2-32.

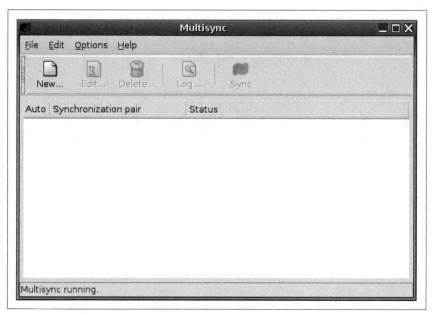

Figure 2-32. Launching Multisync for the first time

Testing Multisync. To make sure that Multisync is working properly, you should configure the backup plug-in and do a test sync with it. Click the New button, and the Synchronization Pair dialog will appear, as shown in Figure 2-33.

Specify Ximian Evolution 2 as the first plug-in and Backup as the second (see Figure 2-33). Give this pair a name, and then click and set the Options for each plug-in. For Evolution, you need to specify which calendar, address book, and task categories to sync. For Backup, you need to specify a backup directory (this appears on the Options tab of the Backup plug-in options dialog). You can then dismiss the Synchronization Pair dialog by clicking OK, which returns you to the main Multisync window. Click once to select the pair you just created, and then click the Sync button. The sync should go quickly, depending on how many contacts, tasks, and appointments you have. Once it's finished, open a shell or Nautilus window and navigate to whichever backup directory you specified in the Backup options. You should see some new files there:

```
bjepson@ubuntoo2:~$ cd backup/
bjepson@ubuntoo2:~/backup$ ls -l
total 8
-rw-r--r-- 1 bjepson bjepson  26 2006-02-07 16:14 backup_entries
-rw-r--r-- 1 bjepson bjepson 422 2006-02-07 16:14 multisync1139346850-0
```

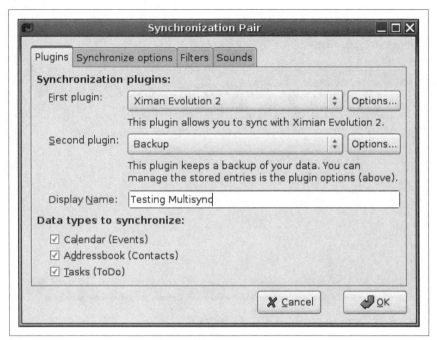

Figure 2-33. Testing Multisync with the backup plug-in

Syncing to the Pocket PC. Return to the Multisync main window and click Add again. This time, set up a Synchronization Pair between Evolution and the SynCE plug-in. Just as you did with the earlier pair, click Options (next to Evolution) to configure which categories to synchronize (the SynCE plug-in has no options). Click OK to dismiss the dialog and return to the Multisync main window. Click to select the Evolution/SynCE pair and click the Sync button.

If all went well, your Pocket PC and Evolution will be in sync. Click the Log button to see what happened. In Figure 2-34, you can see that two entries were copied successfully from the Pocket PC to Evolution.

Each time you want to sync, you'll need to start *dccm* (or keep it running in the background), plug in the Pocket PC, and run sudo synce-serial-start. Then you can launch Multisync and synchronize. To disconnect, run killall -HUP dccm and unplug the Pocket PC.

Install Pocket PC Software

Pocket PC software usually comes in one of two forms: a self-installing *.exe* file designed to be run under Windows, or a *.cab* (cabinet) file that contains

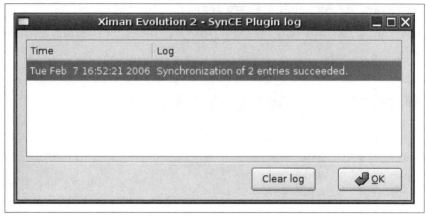

Figure 2-34. The Multisync log after synchronizing with a Pocket PC

ready-to-run binaries for your Pocket PC. If you're stuck with an *.exe* file, no need to worry. The *orange* package is available in the *universe* repository [Hack #60] and will extract the *.cab* files for you:

```
$ orange PocketVCSSetup.exe
squeezing out: /home/bjepson/pocketvcs.arm.cab
squeezing out: /home/bjepson/pocketvcs.mips.cab
squeezing out: /home/bjepson/pocketvcs.sh3.cab
-------
3 files
```

Once you have the *.cab* file (either downloaded from a web site or extracted using *orange*), you can install it onto your Pocket PC. Most modern Pocket PCs are of the ARM variety, but you can use *synce-pstatus* to find out for sure:

```
$ synce-pstatus | grep ^Processor
Processor architecture: 5 (ARM)
Processor type:         2577 (StrongARM)
```

Then you can use *synce-install-cab* to install the *.cab* file for the appropriate architecture:

```
$ synce-install-cab pocketvcs.arm.cab
Copying file 'pocketvcs.arm.cab' to device...
File copy of 1660980 bytes took 0 minutes and 6 seconds, that's 276830
bytes/s.
Installing 'pocketvcs.arm.cab'...
```

After the file is copied over, you will see an installer run on your Pocket PC. You may be prompted for additional information. You can use the *synce-list-programs* and *synce-remove-program* utilities to list and remove programs you've installed on the Pocket PC.

Accessing the Pocket PC's Filesystem

You can work with files on the Pocket PC using the utilities listed in Table 2-1.

Table 2-1. Utilities for working with the Pocket PC filesystem

Utility	Description
synce-pcp	Copy a file
synce-pls	List files
synce-pmkdir	Create a directory
synce-pmv	Move/rename a file
synce-prmdir	Remove a directory

For example, the PocketVCS application (*http://pocketvcs.emuunlim.com*) isn't much good without some games. As you can see, it doesn't come with any:

```
$ synce-pls "/My Documents/PocketVCS/"
AC--------     444646  Tue 11 Mar 2003 04:19:22 PM EST  PocketVCS.pro
```

To actually manipulate a file (copy, remove, etc.), you need to prefix it on the remote filesystem with a colon (:). Here's how to copy the free Oystron (*http://www.io.com/~nickb/atari/oystron.html*) over to the Pocket PC:

```
$ synce-pcp OYSTR29.BIN ":/My Documents/PocketVCS/OYSTR29.BIN"
File copy took less than one second!
```

As you can see, the file is over there and ready to play:

```
$ synce-pls "/My Documents/PocketVCS/"
AC--------       4096  Thu 01 Jul 2004 04:56:26 AM EDT  OYSTR29.BIN
AC--------     444646  Tue 11 Mar 2003 04:19:22 PM EST  PocketVCS.pro
```

Troubleshooting

If you have trouble with your Pocket PC, make sure that the *ipaq* module was loaded correctly and examine the output of *dmesg* to ensure that the Pocket PC was detected and the serial link was established.

If your Pocket PC and Evolution don't seem to be talking, go back to the terminal that's running *dccm* and make sure that it has recognized your Pocket PC and established a connection to it. If they aren't talking, try stopping the connection and reconnecting. If `killall -HUP dccm` doesn't reset the connection, try `sudo synce-serial-abort`. Pocket PCs are notorious for getting confused about things, so if you find that it's impossible to connect after that point, you might want to reset your Pocket PC. Heck, you might even need to reboot your computer if things get really confused.

If you still have problems, visit the SynCE web site (*http://synce.sourceforge.net*) for documentation and other troubleshooting information.

—Brian Jepson

Customize the Right-Click Contextual Menu

Write your own scripts to perform custom actions when you right-click on a file, folder, or the desktop, and add templates to make document creation quick and painless.

Right-clicking on items on the desktop or in the Nautilus file browser pulls up a contextual menu that allows you to perform operations directly on the item. But you're not limited to just the default options: you can add template documents and scripts to the menu for easy access with a single click.

Easy-Access Templates

Right-clicking on the desktop or in the background of a Nautilus window brings up a Create Document menu item, which normally includes only an "Empty File" item. If you select Empty File, a new file called *new file* will be created, and you can rename it to anything you like. However, the new file is just a totally empty file. Creating a document this way is essentially the same as running:

```
$ touch "new file"
```

and about as useful.

However, it's easy to add your own templates to the menu. Create a directory called *Templates* in your home directory:

```
$ mkdir ~/Templates
```

Any document you place in that directory will now be available through the Create Document contextual menu. If the menu becomes large, you can group items into submenus by placing them in subdirectories within *Templates*.

HTML developers can put a file called *HTML File.html* in this directory (it will appear as "HTML File" on the Create Document menu) and fill it with the skeleton of an HTML file. If you create a lot of corporate documents using OpenOffice.org templates, copy the templates in, and you'll be able to start a new document in any location by just right-clicking and selecting the template.

If you do not see your new templates appear in the menu right away, just log out of GNOME and log back in again.

Custom Scripts

You can also execute custom scripts directly from the contextual menu by placing your scripts into a special directory located inside your home directory: *.gnome2/nautilus-scripts/*. Any script you place in that location can be accessed by right-clicking on a file or window and selecting it from the Scripts submenu. (The Scripts menu will not be available unless you have some scripts installed.)

When a script is executed via the contextual menu, it is passed a number of environment variables and usually a number of arguments so it can optionally act on the files you have selected. If you execute the script from the context of a local folder on your computer, it will be passed the names of all selected files as arguments. If you execute the script from the context of a remote folder [Hack #20], such as a Nautilus window showing web or FTP content, no arguments will be passed to it.

Four environment variables are also set, which you can access from within the script:

NAUTILUS_SCRIPT_SELECTED_FILE_PATHS
> Newline-delimited paths for selected files if they are local

NAUTILUS_SCRIPT_SELECTED_URIS
> Newline-delimited URIs for selected files

NAUTILUS_SCRIPT_CURRENT_URI
> URI for current location

NAUTILUS_SCRIPT_WINDOW_GEOMETRY
> Position and size of the current window

There are even packages for various prewritten script collections, such as the Nautilus Subversion Management Scripts and Nautilus Audio Convert packages, which allow you to perform Subversion actions and convert audio file formats by right-clicking on files:

```
$ sudo apt-get install nautilus-script-collection-svn \
  nautilus-script-audio-convert
```

> Not seeing the Scripts menu when you right-click? That may be because Nautilus doesn't think you have any scripts. To give it a heads-up, select Go → Location, type ~/.gnome2/nautilus-scripts into the location bar, and press Enter. Next time you right-click on a file or directory, you should see the Scripts menu.

As a simple example, you could place the following into *~/.gnome2/nautilus-scripts/Terminal* to give you easy access to a terminal from the contextual menu:

```
#!/bin/sh
gnome-terminal
```

This will open a terminal with the current directory set to the directory that encloses whatever you right-clicked on. So, if you right-clicked on the icon for *~/foo*, you'd get a terminal whose current working directory was *~*. But suppose you right-click on a directory. The following Terminal script will check each item in NAUTILUS_SCRIPT_SELECTED_FILE_PATHS, and if it finds a directory, it will cd to it and open the terminal there. Otherwise, it will just open the terminal in the directory that contains the item you clicked on:

```
#!/bin/sh
for d in $NAUTILUS_SCRIPT_SELECTED_FILE_PATHS; do
  if [ -d $d ]; then
    cd $d
    gnome-terminal
    exit
  fi
done
gnome-terminal
```

More complex uses could be to encrypt a selected file using GPG, set a selected image as the desktop background, or send a selected file as an email attachment. For a collection of a variety of scripts specifically designed for use in the contextual menu, visit *http://g-scripts.sourceforge.net*.

HACK #25 Download and Share Files with the Best P2P Software

File sharing is here to stay, and Ubuntu provides some powerful tools that enable users to join the revolution.

Peer-to-peer is huge and getting bigger all the time. Linux users don't have to be left out of all the excitement. In fact, we have a huge variety of P2P apps and networks from which to choose. In this hack, I'm going to show you how to install several different P2P apps; using them, however, will be up to you. And be sensible about what you share, OK? I don't want any large organizations, whose job is protecting dying cartels, suing you.

BitTorrent

When it comes to P2P, first and foremost on any serious Linux user's machine is BitTorrent, the fabulous technology developed by Bram Cohen

that makes downloading ISOs and other huge collections of files easy, fast, and stable.

> Don't know how BitTorrent works or what makes it special? See the Wikipedia article at *http://en.wikipedia.org/wiki/ Bittorrent*. Also at Wikipedia, there is an excellent comparison of the various BitTorrent clients (*http://en.wikipedia.org/ wiki/Comparison_of_BitTorrent_clients*).

There are oodles of BitTorrent apps, and they can all be classified as either command-line or GUI-based. You should know about both, since they each have their purposes. If I'm looking for something quick and dirty, I use the command line; if I want a lot more info and control, I use a GUI.

Command line. You probably already have BitTorrent installed on your copy of Ubuntu, which the following command will confirm:

```
$ whereis bittorrent
bittorrent: /usr/share/bittorrent
```

If you don't have it on your computer, run the following:

```
$ sudo apt-get install bittorrent
```

Accept any dependencies if they're requested, and now you're ready to roll.

To test the software, try downloading a Linux ISO image. Open Firefox and head over to *http://linuxtracker.org*, which tracks many different Linux distros, all available via BitTorrent. Find a distro that intrigues you, and click on the little floppy-disk icon. When Firefox asks you where to save the *.torrent* file, pick a location on your hard drive and save it (Firefox may just go ahead and drop it in the *Desktop* directory). In my case, I'll use *~/iso*, a directory in my home for ISO images. Close Firefox, open your terminal, cd to the directory containing the *.torrent*, and then use the text-mode BitTorrent client (*btdownloadcurses*) to download the file:

```
$ cd ~/iso
$ ls
KANOTIX-2006-CeBIT-RC3.iso.torrent
$ btdownloadcurses --responsefile KANOTIX-2006-CeBIT-RC3.iso.torrent
```

Once BitTorrent starts up, you'll see information about the progress of your download (and upload, since BitTorrent also shares whatever you download with other users; if you want to limit upload speed, use the --max_upload_ rate *SPEED* option on the command line, replacing *SPEED* with the speed in kilobytes per second):

```
| file:    KANOTIX-2006-CeBIT-RC3.iso
| size:    694,765,568 (662.58 MiB)
```

```
| dest:     /home/scott/iso/KANOTIX-2006-CeBIT-RC3.iso
| progress: ##_____ _
| status:   finishing in 1:09:25 (3.5%)
| dl speed: 193.6 KB/s
| ul speed: 0.5 KB/s
| sharing:  0.007  (0.2 MB up / 28.5 MB down)
| seeds:    13 seen now, plus 0.882 distributed copies
| peers:    1 seen now, 85.7% done at 56.2 kB/s
```

If you have a URL instead of a torrent file, use a slightly different command:

```
$ btdownloadcurses --url "http://linuxtracker.org/download. ⏎
php?id=1624&name=KANOTIX-2006-CeBIT-RC3.iso.torrent"
```

The same progress information will appear, allowing you to follow along with the progress of BitTorrent. Just leave your terminal open until your download finishes. In order to give something back to your fellow Bit-Torrent users, it's a good idea to leave everything running until your upload is equal to your download. When you're ready to stop BitTorrent, just press Q to quit.

> For more information about using BitTorrent on the command line, use man bittorrent. There are actually a lot of different options you can use to customize BitTorrent exactly to your needs.

GUI. There are lots of good BitTorrent GUIs out there, but Azureus is probably the best—with the most features, constant updates, and a dedicated development team. Before you can use the program, however, you need to install Java **[Hack #18]**, since Azureus requires it. (Sun's licensing, however, makes it impossible for Ubuntu to include the official Java Runtime Environment in its repositories.)

After you've installed Java, download Azureus from *http://azureus. sourceforge.net/*. Extract the file somewhere, such as */opt*:

```
$ cd /opt/
$ sudo tar xvfj /home/bjepson/Desktop/Azureus_2.4.0.2_linux.tar.bz2
```

You can now run Azureus by executing /opt/azureus/azureus. As you can see in Figure 2-35, it's a program that gives you an enormous amount of data about the files you're downloading and sharing.

For more on this great app, check out an article I wrote for *Linux Magazine* titled "Azureus: A Better Way to BitTorrent" (*http://www.linux-mag.com/ content/view/1923/43/*). It'll give you some tips when it comes to using Azureus that you should find useful.

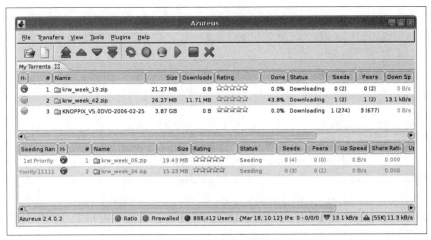

Figure 2-35. Azureus is a full-featured, powerful P2P app

aMule and eDonkey2000

aMule is a P2P client for the eDonkey2000 (or ed2k) network, which, according to Wikipedia, is the most widely used P2P network in the world (see *http://en.wikipedia.org/wiki/EDonkey_network* for that statistic, as well as some other important information you should read if you plan to use the ed2k network). You can install aMule using *apt-get*, since it is part of Ubuntu's *universe* repository.

Make sure that the *universe* repository [Hack #60] is enabled, and then enter the following:

```
$ sudo apt-get install amule
```

You'll be asked if you want to install some other packages that aMule needs, so go ahead and say yes. When *apt* finishes, you can start aMule by going to the K menu → Internet → aMule (if you use KDE) or Applications → Internet → aMule (if you use GNOME). The program will start up, as you can see in Figure 2-36.

aMule is running, but there's a lot more to do. To configure and use aMule, start with the "aMule wiki" (*http://www.amule.org/wiki/index.php/Main_Page*), especially the Getting Started page (*http://www.amule.org/wiki/index.php/ Getting_Started*). Another great source of help is the aMule forums (*http:// www.amule.org/amule/index.php*). Try out aMule: you really can find just about anything there.

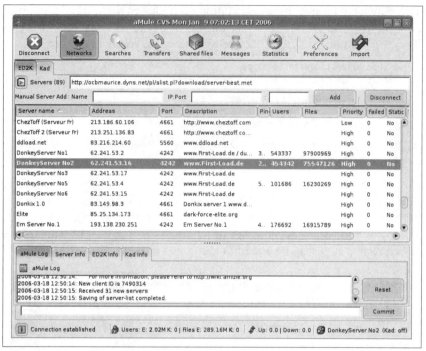

Figure 2-36. Running aMule

LimeWire and Gnutella

One of the first solutions to the centralized-server problem posed by Napster was the Gnutella network (for more info, see *http://en.wikipedia.org/wiki/Napster* and *http://en.wikipedia.org/wiki/Gnutella*). Today, there are many Gnutella clients available for Linux users, but one of the best is undoubtedly LimeWire. There are two versions of LimeWire: the pay version (which is $18.00 for six months of updates) and the free version, which will constantly bother you to upgrade to the pay version but is otherwise adware- and spyware-free.

To get the free version, point your web browser to *http://www.limewire.com/LimeWireSoftLinux*, and you should be prompted to accept a download. It's an RPM file, which normally won't work on a Debian-based distro like Ubuntu, but don't worry. You're going to use a wonderful program called Alien to convert the RPM into something you can use on your distro. First, you'll need to install *alien*:

```
$ sudo apt-get install alien
```

You may have to approve a few additional packages that satisfy dependencies, so go ahead and do so. Once *alien* is in place, you can use it to transform the RPM into a DEB suitable for installing on your Ubuntu box:

```
$ sudo alien LimeWireLinux.rpm
limewire-free_4.10.9-1_i386.deb generated
```

Now you can install the LimeWire DEB:

```
$ sudo dpkg -i limewire-free_4.10.9-1_i386.deb
```

As a bonus, you now have a DEB that you can use on other Ubuntu machines under your control, or you can pass it along to friends.

To use LimeWire, go to the K menu → Internet → LimeWire (for KDE) or Applications → Internet → LimeWire (for GNOME). LimeWire will open and ask you a few questions to get started, and then you can begin using it to search for goodies, as you can see in Figure 2-37. (Regrettably, some of the search results appear to be unauthorized copies of books and other material.)

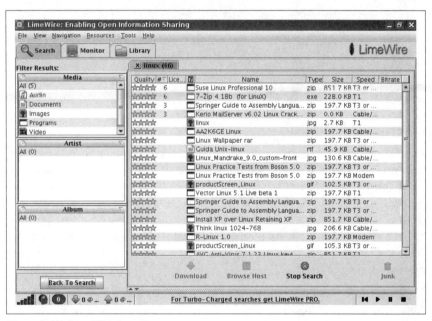

Figure 2-37. LimeWire in action

LimeWire is a powerful program that connects to a large and popular network, so you should be able to have a lot of fun with it.

Other P2P Apps

I've shown you programs for many of the popular P2P networks, but there are many others out there, and it seems like new networks and programs

pop up all the time. A great way to keep up-to-date with this growing technology is through the Wikipedia article "Comparison of file sharing applications" (*http://en.wikipedia.org/wiki/Comparison_of_P2P_applications*). If you see one that looks interesting, do a Google search for that app or network, followed by the word "Ubuntu"; so, for instance, if a new P2P app appeared named "arglebargle," you'd query Google for *arglebargle ubuntu* to see if there was any Ubuntu-specific info available. Just remember: be careful with what you share!

—Scott Granneman

Make Your Own PDFs

Are you used to using the "Print to PDF" feature in Adobe Acrobat? Here's how you can make your own PDF files using a similar technique.

A very handy feature that's included in the Mac OS X operating system is the ability to "print" a PDF file from any application. Windows can also do this, via Adobe Acrobat. However, with the addition of a single package and a little bit of tweaking, you can get the same capability for free on Ubuntu Linux.

Installing CUPS-PDF

The key to getting PDF printing enabled is in the package *cups-pdf*, which is in the *universe* repository [Hack #60]. Use *apt-get* from a terminal window to install the *cups-pdf* package:

```
bill@lexington:~$ sudo apt-get install cups-pdf
Password:
Reading package lists... Done
Building dependency tree... Done
The following NEW packages will be installed
  cups-pdf
0 upgraded, 1 newly installed, 0 to remove and 34 not upgraded.
Need to get 23.4kB of archives.
After unpacking 147kB of additional disk space will be used.
Get: 1 http://us.archive.ubuntu.com dapper/universe cups-pdf 2.0.3-1 [23.
4kB]
Fetched 23.4kB in 0s (31.2kB/s)
Selecting previously deselected package cups-pdf.
(Reading database ... 105713 files and directories currently installed.)
Unpacking cups-pdf (from .../cups-pdf_2.0.3-1_i386.deb) ...
Setting up cups-pdf (2.0.3-1) ...
 * Stopping Common Unix Printing System: cupsd              [ ok ]
 * Starting Common Unix Printing System: cupsd    ...done.
```

After the installation of *cups-pdf* is complete, the CUPS configuration file requires a small edit to enable PDF printing. From a terminal window, run:

```
bill@lexington:~$ sudo gedit /etc/cups/cupsd.conf
```

Find the line that says RunAsUser Yes and change it to RunAsUser No, and then save the file and exit *gedit*. Next, you'll need to restart CUPS to make the configuration change effective:

```
bill@lexington:~$ sudo /etc/init.d/cupsys restart
 * Stopping Common Unix Printing System: cupsd    [ ok ]
 * Starting Common Unix Printing System: cupsd    ...done.
```

Configuring CUPS for the PDF Printer

Now you must tell CUPS to use the newly installed *cups-pdf* package. Click on the System menu; select Administration and then Printing. Double-click on New Printer to start the "Add a Printer" wizard. Ensure that Local Printer is selected under the printer type and that "Use a Detected Printer" is selected, with PDF Printer highlighted in the list below (see Figure 2-38). Click on Forward to proceed.

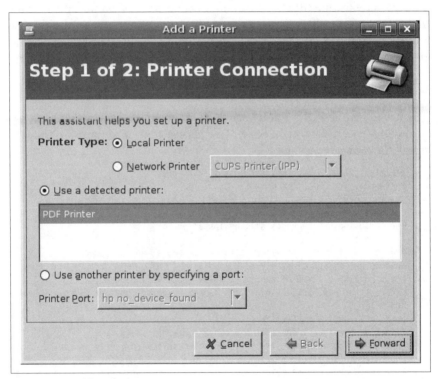

Figure 2-38. Adding the PDF printer

On the next screen, select Generic under the Manufacturer field (see Figure 2-39). Pull down the Model pull-down and select "postscript color printer." Click on Apply to commit the changes.

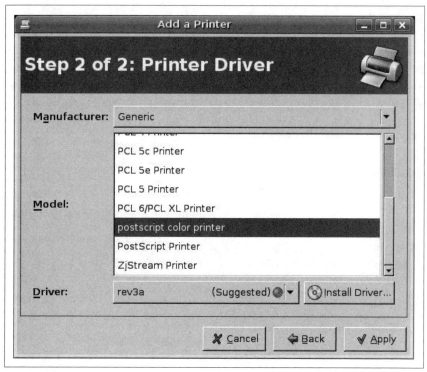

Figure 2-39. Specifying the PostScript driver

Using Your New PDF Printer

Using the new PDF printer is simple: from any application, use that application's native printing facility and select "postscript-color-printer" as your printer. The printer driver will automatically create a PDF and put it in a PDF subdirectory within your home directory. The filename will probably be something like *job_1-untitled_document.pdf*. That's it, it's just that easy! Who needs Acrobat?

Blog with Ubuntu

#27 Blogging is all the rage, and you can update your blog from Ubuntu using the Drivel blog client.

Blogging has become a very popular activity as of late; there's even been an O'Reilly book about it (*Essential Blogging* by Cory Doctorow et al.). Lots of people have LiveJournals or maintain their own blog servers. Most blogs have their own web-based administrative interfaces, but if you're not online, you can't update your blog. That's where a blog client comes in: it allows you to write blog posts offline and upload them when you're ready. There is a very good blog client called Drivel in the *universe* repository, which is very easy to configure and use.

Installing Drivel

Thanks to *apt-get*, Drivel is extremely easy to install (you need to have the *universe* repository enabled **[Hack #60]**). Simply run the following command from a terminal window:

```
bill@lexington:~$ sudo apt-get install drivel
Reading package lists... Done
Building dependency tree... Done
The following NEW packages will be installed
  drivel
0 upgraded, 1 newly installed, 0 to remove and 34 not upgraded.
Need to get 353kB of archives.
After unpacking 1487kB of additional disk space will be used.
Get: 1 http://us.archive.ubuntu.com dapper/universe drivel 2.0.2-5 [353kB]
Fetched 353kB in 1s (191kB/s)
Selecting previously deselected package drivel.
(Reading database ... 105636 files and directories currently installed.)
Unpacking drivel (from .../drivel_2.0.2-5_i386.deb) ...
Setting up drivel (2.0.2-5) ...
```

There will be a new menu entry for Drivel created in the Applications menu in the Internet section. Simply click on that entry to start Drivel.

Configuring and Using Drivel

Upon starting Drivel for the first time, you'll be presented with the main Drivel dialog box, which is where you'll need to configure the program. Enter your username, password, and server address into the appropriate fields in the dialog, and select your journal type from the drop-down menu. (If you're using a Movable Type or Movable Type–compatible blog such as

Wordpress, make sure to put the path to your *mt-xmlrpc.cgi* file in the Server Address field.) Click on Log In (see Figure 2-40), and Drivel will hook up to your blog and pull down an index of your latest blog posts.

Figure 2-40. Drivel's splash and login screen

Now Drivel's ready for you to make your first post (see Figure 2-41)! Fill in a subject line for your post, and type some content in the big body field. When you click Post, Drivel will upload the post to your blog, where it'll be made available to the whole world. The "Show more options" arrow will bring down a pull-down dialog where you can select which category you want your post to be categorized in, if your blog supports categories.

Drivel also supports different fonts and font effects via the Format menu. It will also automatically construct image links for you, although you'll have to

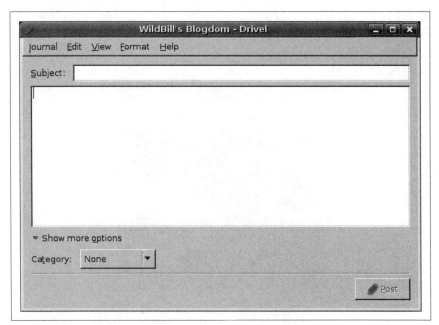

Figure 2-41. Drivel's main window

upload the image (in the correct size) to your blog outside of Drivel. Drivel also makes it easy to call up old blog entries and edit them if necessary; simply click on the Journal menu and select Recent Entries to see the last few entries you've written.

In all, Drivel's one of those small applications that does one thing, and does it well. Give it a test-drive and see if it can't help you manage your blog.

## CHAPTER THREE

Multimedia

Hacks 28–37

A modern computer can be a nifty little entertainment center; it has fast video, stereo speakers, probably plenty of disk space for movies and videos. So, how come Ubuntu doesn't know what to do when you insert a DVD or double-click on a video or audio file?

The fundamental problem is that there are some critical pieces to the multimedia puzzle that Ubuntu can't distribute in all jurisdictions, so you need to go out and get those pieces yourself. Fortunately, Ubuntu makes it easy for you to install those bits once you do obtain them. In this chapter, you'll learn how to get Ubuntu to support more multimedia formats, play DVDs, and even let you buy music online.

For care and feeding of your multimedia collection, you'll need to eventually work with optical discs. Whether you want to take a CD you purchased and rip it down into MP3 files, create a personalized remix CD, or burn a movie to DVD, the hacks in this chapter have you covered.

 ### HACK #28 Install Multimedia Plug-ins

Music and video files come in a wide variety of exotic formats. Learn how to locate and install the plug-ins you need to view or listen to them.

On some Linux distributions, getting all of your multimedia files to play seems like it requires all sorts of command-line voodoo. One thing that sets Ubuntu apart is just how easy it is to grab all of the packages you need to play multimedia content. In this hack, we will walk you through the necessary steps so that once you are finished, Ubuntu will happily play just about any media file you throw at it.

Tweak Your Repository List

Many of the multimedia packages you need to install do not reside in the default Ubuntu repository. To get these packages, you will need to add the *universe* and *multiverse* repositories to Ubuntu. If you haven't done so yet, check out "Modify the List of Package Repositories" [Hack #60] for information about these repositories and how to add them. Once you have added the repositories, be sure to update your list of packages within your package-management tool before proceeding.

Install General-Purpose Libraries and Tools

There are a number of basic libraries and multimedia tools you need to install to get the best support for your multimedia files. These include libraries for MP3 and Ogg Vorbis playback, as well as media players and other tools. If you use Synaptic, select *totem-xine* from the GNOME Desktop Environment (*universe*) category, *vorbis-tools* from the Multimedia category, *sox* from the Multimedia (*universe*) category, *faad* and *lame* from the Multimedia (*multiverse*) category, *imagemagick* from the Graphics category, and finally *ffmpeg* and *mjpegtools* from the Graphics (*universe*) category. Or, if you use *apt-get*, type:

```
$ sudo apt-get install totem-xine vorbis-tools sox faad lame \
    imagemagick ffmpeg mjpegtools
```

Install Gstreamer Libraries

Gstreamer is a new plug-in-based approach to multimedia playback. GNOME uses Gstreamer for much of its own multimedia playback, and, while it is still under heavy development, you will still want to install a number of Gstreamer libraries for GNOME. If you use Synaptic as your package management tool, select the *gstreamer0.8-plugins-multiverse* package from the Libraries (*multiverse*) category; *gstreamer0.8-ffmpeg*, *gstreamer0.8-mad*, and *gstreamer0.8-plugins* from the Libraries (*universe*) category; and *gstreamer0.8-lame* from the Multimedia (*multiverse*) category, and apply your changes. Alternatively, if you use *apt-get*, type:

```
$ sudo apt-get install gstreamer0.8-plugins-multiverse \
    gstreamer0.8-ffmpeg gstreamer0.8-mad gstreamer0.8-plugins \
    gstreamer0.8-lame
```

> If version 0.8 of these Gstreamer libraries is not available, search your package repository to see if a new version is available (for example, if you are using *apt*, run the command apt-cache search gstreamer).

Once you have installed all the Gstreamer libraries, open a terminal and type:

```
$ gst-register-0.8
```

to register all of the Gstreamer plug-ins on your system.

Install Codecs of Ambiguous Legality

There are a number of multimedia formats that are encumbered by special licenses that require the user to leverage Windows codec libraries on their Linux system to play back the file. Some of these include QuickTime and Windows Media formats. In certain countries, it may be illegal to play files via these codecs, so open up your checkbook, call up your lawyer, and have a chat before proceeding. Then, open a terminal window and grab a copy of the *w32codecs .deb* file from *ftp://ftp.nerim.net/debian-marillat/pool/main/w/w32codecs/* and install the *.deb*:

```
$ wget ftp://ftp.nerim.net/debian-marillat/pool/main/w/w32codecs/w32codecs_ ⏎
20050412-0.0_i386.deb
$ sudo dpkg -i w32codecs_20050412-0.0_i386.deb
```

If for some reason that site isn't available, you can also track down the *w32codecs* packages from the official MPlayer page at *http://mplayerhq.hu*.

> For information on setting up your computer to play encrypted DVDs, read "Play DVDs" **[Hack #30]**.

Watch Videos
#29

While the default Totem video player in Ubuntu is great, it's hard to beat MPlayer in terms of flexibility, configurability, and features.

Every once in a while, a tool comes along in Linux that impresses you in almost every respect with its flexibility. MPlayer is one of those tools. When it comes to video and audio playback, think of MPlayer as your universal translator. It can play basically any audio or video format you throw at it (provided it has the libraries available), in just about any container you throw at it. For instance, it can play DVDs from the disc, an image of the disc, or even just the VOBs from the disc. Of course, depending on your taste, there is one downside: by default, MPlayer is a command-line program. There is a graphical frontend for MPlayer for those interested, called *gmplayer*, or you can just use the default Ubuntu video player, Totem. This hack discusses the basics of how to play multimedia files with MPlayer from the command line.

Install MPlayer

The first step to using MPlayer is to install it and the codecs it needs. If you haven't already followed the steps in "Install Multimedia Plug-ins" [Hack #28], do that first to get all of the codecs you'll need. Next, use your preferred packaging tool and install the *mplayer* package that matches your CPU architecture. If you use *apt-get*, type:

```
$ sudo apt-get install mplayer-686
```

Replace *686* with 386, 586, k6, k7, g4, g5, etc., depending on your processor. To see a list of the different processor options, type:

```
$ apt-cache search mplayer
```

Use MPlayer

With MPlayer installed, basic file playback is as simple as opening a terminal and typing:

```
$ mplayer file.avi
```

The console will immediately fill with a lot of different output. This can be useful because MPlayer is telling you what information it can figure out about the file you passed to it, along with information about how it will try to play it. MPlayer should also display the video in a new window and immediately start playback. Back in the console, you will see output scroll by as MPlayer updates you on which frame is playing and how far along MPlayer is in the video.

MPlayer provides an extensive list of key bindings so that you can control playback. The manpage lists all of these options; Table 3-1 lists some of the more commonly used ones.

Table 3-1. Mplayer keybindings

Keys	Function
Left and right arrows	Seek backward/forward 10 seconds
Up and down arrows	Seek backward/forward 1 minute
Page Up and Page Down	Seek backward/forward 10 minutes
< and >	Move backward/forward in playlist
p, Space	Pause movie (pressing again unpauses)
q, Esc	Stop playing and quit
+ and −	Adjust audio delay by +/− 0.1 seconds
/,9 and *,0	Decrease/increase volume
m	Mute sound
f	Toggle full-screen
t	Toggle stay-on-top

Most of these key bindings are pretty self-explanatory, but the + and − options to adjust the audio delay are worth further discussion. Sometimes when you create your own videos or convert videos between formats, the audio and video fall out of sync. This can be very frustrating when you are watching a movie, but with MPlayer, you can tweak the audio with the + and − keys. Just hit one of the keys a few times and see whether you have improved or worsened the sync problems, and then adjust until the video and audio is completely in sync.

The full-screen key binding (f) won't necessarily scale the video to fill up the entire screen. Whether the video scales depends on the video output option you select for MPlayer.

MPlayer is truly a universal multimedia playback tool, and the next sections list some examples for playing back specific video types. For most video files, it is sufficient to simply pass the filename as an argument to *mplayer*, but for special videos such as DVDs, VCDs, and filestreams, things are done slightly differently.

DVD playback. MPlayer has good support for DVD playback; however, one thing it does not support is DVD menus. When you play a DVD with MPlayer, it skips the menu system and everything else up-front and goes right to the movie, which can actually be a good thing if you don't want to sit through the numerous ads and FBI warnings some DVDs have. Most DVDs have a main feature—the movie you purchased—plus several lesser features, such as behind-the-scenes footage or scenes that were cut. In the case of episodic discs like TV box sets, each episode is a different feature. Each of these features is a title, and you can select which title to play when you run *mplayer*. To start playback of the first title on a DVD, type:

```
$ mplayer dvd://1
```

To play other titles, replace 1 with the number of the title you want to play. If you want to play a range of titles, you can specify the range on the command line. For instance, to play titles three through six, type:

```
$ mplayer dvd://3-6
```

You can also specify individual chapters (scenes) or a range of chapters with the -chapter argument. To play chapters four through eight on title one, type:

```
$ mplayer dvd://1 -chapter 4-8
```

MPlayer will attempt to play from */dev/dvd*, but if that device doesn't exist, or you want to point it to a different device, use the -dvd-device argument. The following command will play back from */dev/hdc*:

```
$ mplayer dvd://1 -dvd-device /dev/hdc
```

You can even use the -dvd-device argument to play back directly from a DVD image somewhere on your filesystem:

```
$ mplayer dvd://1 -dvd-device /path/to/dvd.iso
```

It is even possible to use a directory full of VOB files:

```
$ mplayer dvd://1 -dvd-device /path/to/directory/
```

You may also specify language and subtitle options directly from the command line. The -alang option controls the audio language option and can accept multiple languages separated by commas. In that case, MPlayer will try the first language and fall back on the next language if the first isn't available. For instance, to play a movie in Japanese and fall back to English if Japanese isn't available, type:

```
$ mplayer dvd://1 -alang ja,en
```

The -slang option controls which language's subtitles are shown. To show the English subtitles on the above example, type:

```
$ mplayer dvd://1 -alang ja,en -slang en
```

(S)VCD playback. (S)VCD playback in MPlayer is much like DVD playback. Just use vcd:// instead of dvd:// in the command line, with the track to play as an argument. So, to play track one of a VCD, type:

```
$ mplayer vcd://1
```

MPlayer can even play the *.bin* files from (S)VCDs. You don't even need to pass any special options; just point *mplayer* to the *.bin* file to start playback.

Streaming playback. MPlayer supports playback from a number of different audio and video streams. Just pass the URL on the command line:

```
$ mplayer http://example.com/stream.avi
$ mplayer rtsp://example.com/stream
```

Troubleshooting. There are a number of reasons MPlayer may not output your video correctly. If MPlayer has trouble identifying your video, all the video codecs *mplayer* requires may not be installed on your system. "Install Multimedia Plug-ins" [Hack #28] explains how to find and install the various video and audio codecs you need under Linux.

If MPlayer plays the video, but the video output looks strange, you can't see it at all, or playback is very jerky, it's possible that MPlayer is configured to use the wrong video output option for your system. Try passing -vo x11 as an argument to *mplayer* on the command line and see if that lets you at least view the video.

Another reason for jerky video is simply that a system is too slow to play the video well. In this case, MPlayer will warn you in its output that your system is too slow to play the video and will recommend that you add the -framedrop option. This option tells MPlayer to drop video frames if the video can't keep up with the audio on the system.

HACK #30 Play DVDs

Install libraries that allow you to play encrypted DVDs under Ubuntu.

Out of the box, Ubuntu will probably not be able to play most of the DVDs that you own. This isn't because of an oversight on the part of the Ubuntu developers; it's simply because most DVDs you might buy are encrypted with a system called CSS (Content Scrambling System). While video-player packages such as *totem-gstreamer*, *totem-xine*, *xine*, *mplayer*, and *vlc* can all play unencrypted DVDs, to play CSS-encrypted DVDs, you will have to actually circumvent the encryption scheme. (Note that in certain countries circumventing CSS is not legal, so here is a good place to stop reading and phone up your attorney before proceeding.)

Ubuntu actually makes this process very simple. The first step is to install one of the aforementioned video-player packages along with the *libdvdread3* package, if they aren't installed, so use your preferred package-installation tool to do so (see Chapter 6 for different ways to install packages).

 Which video-player package should you install? This is mostly a matter of preference, but the *totem* video player, particularly the *totem-xine* package, is a good one to try first, since it won't require too many extra packages to work and will integrate into the default GNOME desktop environment well.

After you install *libdvdread3*, you must run the script it provides to download and install the *libdvdcss2* libraries you need. Open a terminal and run the following script:

```
$ sudo /usr/share/doc/libdvdread3/examples/install-css.sh
Password:
--20:19:23--  http://www.dtek.chalmers.se/groups/dvd/deb/libdvdcss2_1.2.5-1_
i386.deb
       => `/tmp/libdvdcss.deb'
Resolving www.dtek.chalmers.se... 129.16.30.198
Connecting to www.dtek.chalmers.se|129.16.30.198|:80... connected.
HTTP request sent, awaiting response... 200 OK
Length: 25,178 (25K) [text/plain]

100%[====================================>] 25,178      55.66K/s
```

```
20:19:25 (55.54 KB/s) - `/tmp/libdvdcss.deb' saved [25178/25178]

(Reading database ... 59605 files and directories currently installed.)
Preparing to replace libdvdcss2 1.2.5-1 (using /tmp/libdvdcss.deb) ...
Unpacking replacement libdvdcss2 ...
Setting up libdvdcss2 (1.2.5-1) ...
```

That's all. Now to play a DVD, just insert it into your computer's DVD player. Ubuntu is configured by default to automatically open DVD video with the Totem media player. If you want to toggle that setting, click System → Preferences → Removable Drives and Media, click the Multimedia tab in the window that appears, and check or uncheck the checkbox next to "Play video DVD disks when inserted" (see Figure 3-1). From this window, you can also change the default program used to open DVDs. Just change the default video player from *totem* to your program of choice.

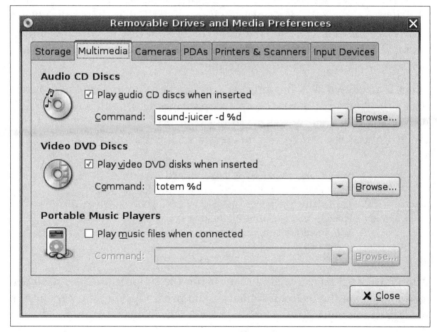

Figure 3-1. The Removable Drives and Media Preferences window

To start Totem manually, click Applications → Sound & Video → Movie Player, then click Movie → Play Disc to open your movie. Totem provides a simple interface to navigate through a movie—with standard Play/Pause, previous track, and next track buttons on the main window, along with a sliding bar you can use to quickly skip through a movie. When you are finished watching the movie, click Movie → Eject or hit Ctrl-E from within Totem.

Buy Songs at the iTunes Music Store

#31 Yes, it's possible to access, buy, and download music from iTMS on Linux.

If you're not averse to spending a little money for a fantastically useful app and to running a proprietary, nonfree program (but then again, if you were, why are you using the DRM-laden iTunes Music Store?), CrossOver Office from CodeWeavers is a great way to get your iTMS fix. As a bonus, you'll also be able to run other Windows-based, proprietary programs, such as Microsoft Word, Excel, PowerPoint, and Internet Explorer, as well as multimedia apps like QuickTime and Shockwave. The advantage of CrossOver is that it makes it really easy to run these Windows programs in Linux, and you won't be skirting the terms of their software licenses. The disadvantage is that CrossOver costs $40, which is, IMHO, a pittance for all that it offers you. If you're not sure if you want to buy the program, you can try it for free for 30 days, which should be plenty of time for you to kick the tires and discover how useful this program really is.

To start with CrossOver, head over to *http://www.codeweavers.com*. Cross-Over Office is featured prominently on the home page, with a big red Try Now button that you should press. Follow the instructions on the page and download the software via FTP, BitTorrent, or HTTP.

After downloading the CrossOver shell script, you need to make it executable and then install it. Both actions are performed as a normal user, without *sudo*:

```
$ chmod 744 install-crossover-standard-demo-5.0.1.sh
$ ./install-crossover-standard-demo-5.0.1.sh
```

A GUI installer will open. Click OK to accept the quite reasonable licensing terms (basically that you won't copy the software and let everyone in the world use it), and then you'll be asked where you wish to install the software. By default, CrossOver will install at */home/<user>/cxoffice*, but I don't like cluttering up my home directory, so I always change that to */home/scott/ .cxoffice*. (There's a dot in front of *cxoffice*, which makes it a hidden directory.) Once that's in place, click Begin Install.

The program installs, and immediately the Introduction Wizard opens so that you can tell CrossOver about your Internet connectivity. Click Next, and you'll be asked if you use an HTTP proxy. Most likely you don't, so click Finish; if you do, enter the correct information and then click Finish.

You're back at the main Setup screen, but now there's a new button: Install Windows Software. Click it, and the Installation Wizard opens, displaying a list of supported Windows software, including various Microsoft, Adobe,

Intuit, and other companies' apps. Scroll down until you see iTunes, and then click Next.

> If it's not clear by now, you are expected to own a license for the software you install, or install freeware like Shockwave and QuickTime. CodeWeavers is a legit company and is not going to provide you with copies of software you're supposed to purchase.

The first screen of the install tells you that CrossOver is going to download and use iTunes 4.9.0, and that you should avoid upgrading. Listen to the folks at CodeWeavers! They test this stuff, and they know what they're talking about.

You're given a choice between the Express and Advanced install; go with the Express unless you absolutely know what you're doing and need the Advanced option. Click Next. CrossOver will download and install iTunes for you, and the whole time Apple's program will think it's running on Windows instead of Linux. I'm not going to walk you through an installation of iTunes, since presumably you're already familiar with how to install (and use) it. It's mostly just Next, Next, Next, anyway.

When CrossOver finishes, you'll reach the end of the Installation Wizard. If you're ready to quit CrossOver, click Finish. Before doing so, you ought to check the box next to "Remove installer files" so you can keep your hard drive tidy. If you had a problem with the installation and you want to help CodeWeavers diagnose the issue, check the box next to "Package log for CodeWeavers support," which saves a logfile detailing the process, so that tech support has some useful info. If you want to place more software on your system, check the box next to "Install more Windows software," which starts the wizard over again. Finally, "View installed associations" shows you what file types are now linked to the program you just installed. It may be handy to see, so feel free to check it.

Now that iTunes is installed on your Ubuntu machine, you'll find a shortcut for it on your desktop, as well as on your K menu (if you're using KDE) or Applications menu (if you're using GNOME). Start up the program, and you can buy as much DRM-laden music as you'd like.

> I'm not really a fan of iTunes, or DRM in general. For my reasons why, see an article titled "The Big DRM Mistake" that I wrote for SecurityFocus, available at *http://www. securityfocus.com/columnists/390.*

If you ever want to uninstall iTunes, go to your K menu or Applications menu, and then to CrossOver → Configuration. Select iTunes, and simply press Repair/Remove.

I've used CrossOver to run a wide variety of software; in fact, I've written several books using the VBA-laden Microsoft Word templates that publishers love so much, and they've run beautifully under CrossOver. You'll find that CrossOver is an incredibly invaluable tool that can already run a lot of important Windows apps, including iTunes, with the list growing all the time. Try it out for 30 days and see what you think.

—Scott Granneman

HACK #32 Get a Grip on CD Ripping

Use the Grip program to automate ripping audio CDs into music files.

The command line is definitely a powerful tool, particularly for automation, but it can also make doing a task like ripping a CD more trouble than it's worth, especially if you plan on tagging the resulting audio with metadata such as ID3 tags. While there are several frontends for command-line tools, Grip, in our opinion, is an excellent example of a GUI frontend that balances the power and configurability of the command line with the ease of use of a GUI interface. After you get to the end of this hack, your CD-ripping process will be so automated that once you start, you won't even have to pick up a mouse.

Install Grip

It is simple to install Grip: just install the *grip* package using your preferred package manager. Grip is a frontend in that, for the most part, it uses other command-line utilities behind the scenes to do all of the work and simply provides an easy-to-use interface to configure the commands it passes down to those tools. Because it is a frontend, Grip can make use of many different command-line CD-ripping and audio-encoding programs, and, as such, it supports ripping to a number of popular formats including MP3, Ogg Vorbis, FLAC, or even a custom encoder of your choosing. This also means that to take advantage of those tools, you will need to already have them installed, but Ubuntu's package manager will take care of the major dependencies.

Configure Ubuntu to Default to Grip

By default, Ubuntu uses a program called Sound Juicer to play audio CDs. This program is fine but lacks a lot of the configurability and power of Grip.

You could manually launch Grip each time you want to use it, but you can make Ubuntu launch it for you whenever it detects that an audio CD has been inserted. To do so, click System → Preferences → Removable Drives and Media to open the "Removable Drives and Media Preferences" window. Then, where it says Command under Audio CD Discs (on the Multimedia tab), replace sound-juicer (and its arguments, if any) with grip.

You may have to log out of and back in to GNOME for this change to take effect.

Configure Grip

Before you rip your first CD, you need to configure Grip. First, launch Grip from Applications → Sound & Video → Grip. Grip's main interface is broken into a number of tabs:

Tracks
> This tab displays the current list of tracks for a CD that has been inserted into the CD player and allows you to check which of the tracks you want to rip. Grip also functions as a CD player, so you can select a particular track from this tab and click the play button at the bottom of the window to play the track.

Rip
> Here, you can see the current progress of any ripping and encoding you have scheduled and start or abort the ripping process.

Config
> Under Config, you will find a number of subtabs that configure how Grip rips and encodes a CD.

Status
> Look here for constantly updated text output for any jobs that have been done. You can look here to see any error messages or other output.

Help
> This tab provides buttons to launch help for different categories, including how to play CDs, rip CDs, and configure Grip.

About
> Here, you'll find information about Grip itself, including the version and a link to the official web site.

To configure Grip, click the Config tab to reveal a number of subtabs that configure different Grip settings. The tabs you are interested in are CD, Rip, Encode, ID3, and DiscDB.

Configure CD options. The first tab, CD, lets you configure your CD device. For the most part, the default settings will work, but for the purposes of

automated ripping, make sure that the "Auto-play on disc insert" option is off. To test whether Grip has the correct CD-ROM device, insert an audio CD and see whether Grip sees and can play it. If not, make sure */dev/cdrom* is pointing to your correct CD-ROM device, often */dev/hdc* or */dev/scd0*.

Configure ripping options. The Rip configuration tab is where things start to get interesting. Because so many people are used to automated programs that turn their CDs into MP3s, they often don't realize that ripping is a two-stage process: first ripping the tracks from the CD into WAV files, and then encoding the tracks to MP3, Ogg, or whatever other format you wish. This tab controls the ripping stage of the process, and most of the options are pretty self-explanatory.

The first subtab, Ripper, lets you configure which CD-ripping program to use. Grip now includes its own version of *cdparanoia* by default, and we recommend that you use it unless you have a good reason not to. *cdparanoia* by default rips more slowly than most other ripping programs (on most of our CD-ROM drives, it rips at 2x), but what it loses in speed, it more than makes up for in accuracy. *cdparanoia* is slow because it is particularly thorough about getting every bit it can from the CD. If you rip with faster but less thorough ripping programs, you may notice pops or gaps in your tracks. Even on many of our scratched-up CDs, *cdparanoia* has been able to recover the track.

Once you choose your CD-ripping program, you can configure it further in the Ripper tab. In the case of *cdparanoia*, you can disable a number of its default options, including what it calls "paranoia" and "extra paranoia"—how thorough it is about reading the CD. We recommend you leave these and the scratch-detection and repair options alone. The primary option in this subtab you should be interested in configuring is the "Rip file format" option. Here, you can tell Grip where to put and how to name the WAV files it rips. Grip uses a number of variables that correspond to metadata from the CD. Table 3-2 lists a number of the common variables and what they represent.

Table 3-2. Grip naming variables

Variable	What it represents
%A	The artist name for the disc
%a	The artist name for the track (useful for multiartist CDs)
%y	The year of the disc
%d	The name of the disc
%t	The track number, zero-filled so that 3 would be shown as 03
%n	The name of the track
%x	The encoded file extension (*mp3* for MP3 files, *ogg* for OGG files, and *wav* for WAV files)

For example, if you stored your MP3s in a directory called *mp3* in your home directory, you might put in the "Rip file format" field:

```
~/mp3/%A/%y-%d/%t-%n.%x
```

Decoded, that line would turn Track 10 of the *London Calling* CD by The Clash, called "The Guns of Brixton," into the file *~/mp3/the_clash/1979-london_calling/10-the_guns_of_brixton.wav*.

 You can use whatever naming scheme you wish for your audio files. We prefer this method because it organizes all our CDs by artist, then by each album sorted by date, then by each track. This way, no matter what audio player we use, by default the tracks are all in order.

With this subtab configured, click the Options subtab to get to other ripping options. There are a few options here that we like to enable, particularly "Auto-rip on insert" and "Auto-eject after rip." With these options enabled, when Grip is running it will automatically start ripping a CD for you when you insert it and then eject it when it's done. This means that once the rest of Grip is configured, you can set up a stack of CDs at your desk, start Grip, insert the first CD, and then minimize it and do something else. When you see that the CD has ejected, you can just replace it with another CD to rip and go on with what you were doing. Grip will handle the rest. It doesn't get much more automated than that!

Configure encoding options. The next main configuration tab is Encode. This tab lets you configure what kind of audio files Grip will encode the WAV files into. The first option, Encoder, lets you choose what encoding program to use. What you choose here depends heavily on what encoding programs you have installed and what kind of audio files you want. For instance, if you want to make MP3s, you will likely choose LAME, mp3encode, or your favorite MP3 encoder. We usually stick with LAME because it is fast and produces decent-quality MP3s. If you want to create Ogg Vorbis files, choose "oggenc." If you want to create FLAC files (a lossless audio codec so there is no degradation in quality), choose "flac." After you have chosen the encoder to use, make sure the encoder executable path points to the location of your encoder (the default should be fine here). The defaults for the next two options, the encoder command line and file extension, should be fine unless you choose to use a special encoder not directly supported by Grip. The next field, "Encode file format," takes the same type of information as the "Rip file format" field in the Rip tab. In fact, if you make sure to use %x as the file extension, you can likely just directly copy and paste from this.

In the Options subtab for Encode, you can configure some specific options for your encoder. Probably the most important option here is the "Encoding bitrate" option, which determines the bitrate at which to encode your audio file if you use a lossy encoding such as MP3 or Ogg. What you put here is largely a matter of taste, although the higher the number, the larger your resulting file will be. In the case of MP3s, some people can't tell the difference between 128 and 256 kilobits per second. For other people, the distinction is great. We usually use 192 or 256 kilobits per second here, but you may want to experiment with the output for your audio files and determine what bitrate is best for you; your choice may vary depending on the type of music you are encoding. In this tab, you also have the option to create an *.m3u* playlist file for each CD you rip and choose where to put it. Generally, the only other option we enable in this subtab is "Delete .wav after encoding." (*.wav* files are quite large, and once Grip has encoded them to MP3 or another format, there's no reason to keep the *.wav* around.)

Configure ID3 options. The next major configuration tab, ID3, lets you control whether Grip inserts ID3 tags into your audio files. Generally, this is a good thing, and you will want all these options enabled unless you want to go back later and manually set ID3 tags—an often tedious process.

Configure DiscDB options. The final configuration tab you might want to configure is the DiscDB tab. This tab lets you configure the primary and secondary CD database servers that Grip will query when you insert a CD. These servers contain information on many CDs, based on CD signatures. When you insert a CD, Grip will query this database and retrieve artist, disc, and track information for the CD so that it can automatically fill out the ID3 tags and name the files appropriately. We would recommend sticking with the default servers listed here unless you know what you are doing. Make sure that the "Perform disc lookups automatically" option is enabled here.

Rip a CD

Once you have configured Grip, the process to rip a CD is rather simple: just insert the CD into the CD-ROM drive. Grip will automatically scan the CD, retrieve the track information from your CD database servers, select all tracks for ripping, and start the ripping and encoding process. You can click on the Rip tab to monitor the progress of both the ripping and encoding to see how far along in the process you are. If for some reason you want to stop the ripping process, click the "Abort Rip and Encode" button.

If you notice that the track information that Grip retrieved is wrong, or if Grip was unable to retrieve the track information at all, abort the ripping and encoding process and then click the pencil icon at the bottom of the window. This will expand the window and provide a number of fields that you can use to fill out artist, title, genre, track name, and other CD information. Choose different tracks from the Tracks tab to change specific information for that track. Once you have finished your changes, you can click the envelope icon to submit your changes to your configured CD database so that the information is available to the next person who rips the CD. Once the changes have been made, select all of the tracks in the Tracks tab, and then go to the Rip tab and click Rip+Encode to restart the ripping process.

As mentioned before, the nice thing about configuring Grip in this way is that you can let it run virtually unattended and just feed it new CDs until all your CDs are ripped—which certainly beats typing long commands and editing ID3 tags by hand!

HACK #33   Burn CDs and DVDs

A few click-and-drag operations are all that separates your data from a CD or DVD.

While USB drives seem to be all the rage for transporting data, it's still hard to beat the price of blank CDs or DVDs. Whether you want to create an archive of some files "just in case," or you want to take some larger files with you to another computer, under Ubuntu the process to make a data CD or DVD only takes a couple of clicks.

To copy data to a CD or DVD, first you need a blank CD or DVD. Insert your blank media into your CD/DVD burner and wait a moment as Ubuntu detects that you have inserted blank media into the drive. Figure 3-2 shows you the default prompt that Ubuntu will present you, where you will be given the choice to make an audio CD [Hack #34], make a data CD, or just ignore the CD. Choose Make Data CD. Ubuntu will now open a special Nautilus window devoted to Data CD and DVD creation.

The CD/DVD Creator Folder is pretty basic, as Figure 3-3 illustrates. Essentially, you have an empty directory into which you can drag and drop files you would like to burn. Probably the easiest thing to do is to click the File menu at the top of the screen and open a new Nautilus window, and then drag files or directories from it into the CD/DVD Creator Folder.

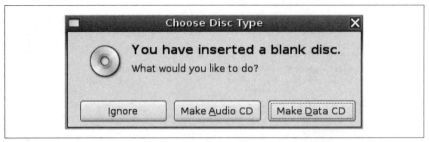

Figure 3-2. The prompt that greets you when you insert a blank CD or DVD

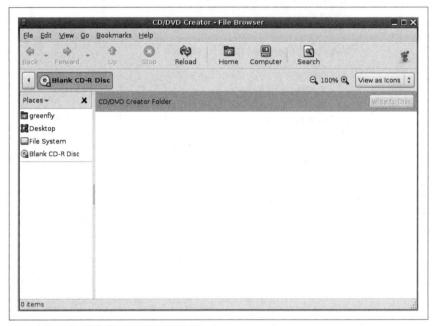

Figure 3-3. The default Nautilus CD/DVD-burning window

Once you have collected all of the files you wish to burn into the folder, click the "Write to Disc" button at the top of the window. A new window will appear that lists some basic CD-burning options in a number of drop-down menus. From here, you can choose between multiple CD burners if your computer has them, assign a name to the disc, view the current size of the disc, and pick the write speed to use.

When you are ready to burn the CD, click the Write button and the CD-burning process will begin. A simple status bar will appear so you can keep track of your disc's progress (see Figure 3-4).

Figure 3-4. The Nautilus Writing Files to CD dialog

If you find the options in the default CD/DVD creator limiting, we recommend checking out the *k3b* package. It isn't installed by default, so you will need to install it with your preferred package manager. K3b offers a number of advanced features and is featured along with the Serpentine audio CD creator in "Automate Audio CD Burning" [Hack #34].

H A C K   Automate Audio CD Burning
#34
Use Serpentine and K3b to burn your own custom audio CD in just a few clicks.

Even with the advent of high-tech hard drives, flash-memory-based media players, and sophisticated peer-to-peer file-sharing software, sometimes the simplest way to take your music with you is on a good old-fashioned CD. After all, many home and car stereos still don't support the playback of MP3s or other audio formats, so if you mix your favorite tracks and burn them to a CD, you can play them just about anywhere. Plus, if your CD breaks, it's quick, easy, and cheap to replace with another burned copy.

Creating a CD used to be a bit of a dark science under Linux and required you to use a number of command-line tools to convert audio files into WAVs if they weren't already WAVs. Then you had to execute another script to burn them onto a CD and, of course, hope that you calculated the song length correctly so your music would all fit on the CD. With Ubuntu, those days are over. Ubuntu offers a number of options for burning audio CDs, but this hack will cover the built-in option Serpentine, and K3b, a very powerful and very user-friendly graphical CD- and DVD-burning tool. Both tools accomplish all of the steps that you would normally have to do on the command line, all within a nice simple interface.

Serpentine is installed by default on your Ubuntu system, so you will only need to get K3b (and its MP3 decoding library, if you want to burn MP3s to disc). To do so, just install the *k3b* and *libk3b2-mp3* packages using your preferred package manager (for example, the command sudo apt-get install k3b libk3b2-mp3 will do the trick). Ubuntu will also need to pull down a number of supporting libraries for K3b, so be patient as everything downloads and installs.

Use Serpentine

To use Serpentine, just insert a blank CD into your CD burner. Ubuntu will pop up a dialog window asking you whether you'd like to burn a data CD, burn an audio CD, or just ignore the CD (see Figure 3-2 in "Burn CDs and DVDs" [Hack #33]). Choose Make Audio CD.

As Figure 3-5 shows, Serpentine's interface is very basic. To add tracks to the CD, either click the Add button to locate audio files on your filesystem or just drag and drop the tracks from your file manager. Serpentine will calculate the remaining time and display it on the main window. Once you are ready to burn the CD, click "Write to Disc," and Serpentine will start the process of converting and burning your tracks to the CD.

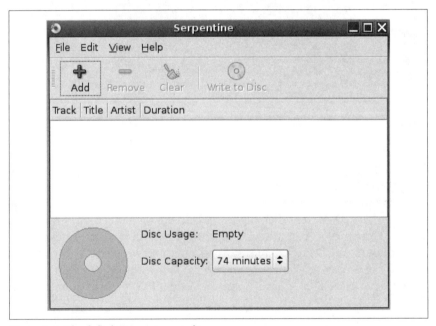

Figure 3-5. The default Serpentine window

Use K3b

To use K3b, either launch it from your application menu or type k3b in a terminal. The screen that initially appears offers some quick links to start common CD-burning projects (Figure 3-6), so click New Audio Project or select
File → New → New Project → New Audio CD Project. The split-screen interface shows you a view of your filesystem at the top of the window and a
view of your CD project at the bottom. To add tracks to your CD, browse
through the top interface to the WAV, MP3, and Ogg Vorbis audio files you
want to add. You can also drag tracks from a CD you have inserted.

Figure 3-6. Main K3b window

As you add tracks, K3b automatically figures out how much space you have
left on the CD and displays it in a progress bar at the bottom of the window. K3b will also read any ID3 tags your music files may have and use the
information to label the tracks on the CD, so that the artist and title will
show up on CD players that support CD-Text. Right-click on a track and
choose Properties to edit any of the text fields, control what portion of the
track to burn to CD, and change the gap length between tracks. If you want
to save the project so you can burn another CD with the same settings at a
future date, click File → Save As to store the project information to your
disk.

Once you have arranged your new CD how you want it, click the Burn button at the bottom-righthand corner of the screen. The dialog that appears
allows you to tweak any last-minute settings for your CD burner, including

write speed, write mode, and which CD burner to use (see Figure 3-7). Unless you have specific needs, the default settings should work just fine. Once you have inserted the CD and are ready to burn, click the final Burn button in this dialog to start the burning process, or the Simulate button to simulate the process without actually writing to the CD. A new status window will appear and give you information on the progress of your burning session, including elapsed time, current track being burned, and other status information.

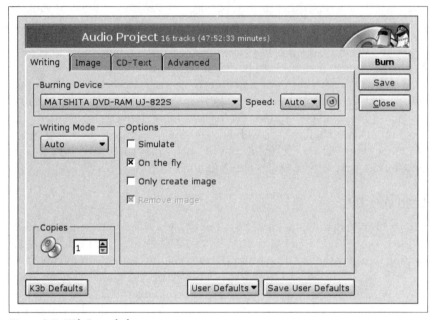

Figure 3-7. K3b Burn dialog

While you can cancel the process at this point by clicking the Cancel button, doing so will almost certainly render your writeable CD useless, or, if it's a rewriteable CD, you will need to blank the CD before writing to it again (in K3b, select Tools → Erase CD-RW).

 ### HACK #35 Rip and Encode DVDs

The acidrip utility gives you access to many of the common mencoder functions so you can use a GUI to rip and encode a DVD to a file.

As with many things under Linux, there are a number of ways to rip and encode a DVD. For instance, some people use the *mencoder* tool (part of the *mplayer* suite) with two-pass encoding to turn VOB files they have extracted

from a DVD into an MPEG4 *.avi* file. This method works great; however, some people are turned off by the thought of doing encoding entirely from the command line. If you want to use *mencoder* to encode a DVD but would rather have a GUI, the *acidrip* utility provides you with a GUI interface for most of the major mencoder options you might want.

Before you install *acidrip*, follow the instructions in "Install Multimedia Plug-ins" [Hack #28] and "Play DVDs" [Hack #30] to make sure that you have all of the multimedia plug-ins you'll need. After that, use your preferred package manager to install the *acidrip* package (it's in the Multiverse subcategory); if you use *apt-get*, type:

```
$ sudo apt-get install acidrip
```

With *acidrip* installed, click Applications → Sound and Video → Acidrip, or type acidrip from the command line to start the program. The default screen that greets you (see Figure 3-8) can be a bit intimidating at first, because it has so many options. For basic ripping, however, there are only a few options you need to worry about, and the nice thing is that *acidrip* will remember your settings for next time. That means that after you have it set up, you can rip multiple DVDs with minimal effort.

Load Your DVD

To rip a DVD, first locate the section on the right side of the window labeled "Video source" and type the path to your DVD in the Path field. If you are ripping directly from a DVD, insert the DVD and type the path to your DVD device (such as */dev/dvd*). If you have already ripped the DVD to the hard drive, type in the path to the directory that contains the DVD's *VIDEO_TS* directory. Click Load, and *acidrip* scans the DVD and displays each title with its playback time. Use the playback time to identify the main title you want to encode (generally the title with the longest playback time, and often the first title on the DVD) and select it.

> If you are unsure of which title is the correct title, select the title and then click the Preview tab. Click the Preview button in that tab, and *acidrip* will use *mplayer* to play that track inside the window. Deselect the "Embed window" checkbox if you want to watch the video in its own window. If you enable any crop settings, you can also preview those here.

Configure Settings

Now click on the General tab on the left side of the window and fill in the "Track title" if *acidrip* didn't automatically detect it for you. By default,

Figure 3-8. The default acidrip window

acidrip uses this field for the final filename. In the Filename field, type in the path where you want *acidrip* to put the final encoded video. The %T in this field is a variable that gets replaced with the contents of the "Track title" field. In the drop-down menu next to the Filename, you can choose whether to give the final video an *.avi* or *.mpg* extension. Underneath that field, you can configure the final file size for the video and whether to split it across multiple files. For instance, if you wanted to fit the video across two CDs, you would set "File size" to 700 and "# Files" to 2.

Those settings should be fine for typical DVD rippings, but *acidrip* provides plenty of other options so that you can configure *mencoder* for special cases. The General tab also lets you configure what codec to use for the audio track, along with whether to include a subtitle in the final video.

The Video tab gives the experienced *mencoder* user access to more advanced options. Here, you can configure which codec to use for the output file and can set the bitrate for the final file by hand. You can also crop the final video or scale it to a different width and height. If you want to add any special pre- or post-filters to *mencoder*, you can also configure those here.

> We noticed that our version of *acidrip* had the pp=de pre-filter enabled by default, which caused an error in *mencoder*. We simply disabled this filter, and *acidrip* worked fine.

The Settings tab lets you configure general *acidrip* options, including what program to use for *mencoder*, *mplayer*, and *lsdvd* (useful if there is more than one instance of these programs in your path) and what directory to use to cache a DVD (if you have that option enabled). From this tab, you can also tell *acidrip* to automatically shut down the computer after it is finished ripping.

Queue and Rip

After you have configured your settings the way you want them, click the Queue button at the bottom of the window to add the job to the queue. The Queue tab displays any queued jobs you have set. This tab can be handy if you want to learn more about the *mencoder* processes *acidrip* uses, because it displays the full commands *mencoder* will run. This can also be good for debugging purposes if *acidrip* fails to start ripping. Copy and paste the *mencoder* lines from the queue to the command line and make note of any errors *mencoder* outputs. You can also queue more than one job, so you can line up a bunch of jobs and leave them running overnight.

Once you finish configuring your job and queue it, click the Start button to start the encoding process. *acidrip* shrinks down to a smaller window and displays its progress, including time left in the current process, encoding speed, and estimated file size. Click the Full View button to go back to the full-sized window. When *acidrip* finishes, it goes back to full view, and you will be able to check out your new video files in the directory you specified.

As mentioned earlier, the nice thing about using *acidrip* over *mencoder* is that you can tweak *acidrip* with your favorite *mencoder* settings a single time and then just concentrate on adding encoding jobs. This helps to eliminate the problem of trying to remember which options to use each time; plus it makes it easier to queue up multiple jobs, one after another.

Create a Video DVD

#36 Use the tovid scripts to automate the conversion of many video formats to DVD.

Before DVD burners and media were relatively inexpensive, creating your own video DVDs was a daunting prospect. Even today, depending on which tools you use, it can still be a daunting prospect under Linux. However, with the tovid set of scripts (*http://tovid.org*), you can easily convert just about any video into a DVD-compatible format.

So you have a video (or a number of videos) that you want to convert into a DVD. The first step is to convert that video into a format compatible with the DVD standard. Although you could use *mencoder* or *transcode* directly to perform this conversion, the number of options involved can quickly get complicated and confusing. Luckily, a great tool, tovid, has been created to solve this problem. The tovid suite is a series of scripts that automate the process of converting a video into a VCD. The scripts involved have basic, easy-to-understand arguments and, because the output shows you the commands that are being executed, you can also use them to learn more about the underlying process.

Install tovid

To install tovid, download the latest release from the official project page at *http://tovid.org*. The main tool in the suite is also called *tovid* and uses the *mplayer*, *mjpegtools*, *ffmpeg*, *mkisofs*, *dvdauthor*, *transcode*, *vcdimager*, and *normalize-audio* packages to perform the video conversion, so you will need to have these packages installed beforehand (you'll need the *universe* and *multiverse* repositories enabled [Hack #60]). For example:

```
$ sudo apt-get install mplayer mjpegtools ffmpeg mkisofs \
    dvdauthor normalize-audio transcode vcdimager
```

Once these requirements are met, download the latest release and untar it:

```
$ tar -xzvf tovid-0.25.tar.gz
```

Now enter the *tovid* source directory that *tar* created and then run the *configure* script inside. This script automates the process of installing tovid on your system, and once it completes, you are ready to start:

```
greenfly@ubuntu:~$ cd tovid-0.25
greenfly@ubuntu:~tovid-0.25$ ./configure
```

The *configure* script will confirm that you have all the required dependencies installed. If you are missing a dependency, check out "Search for Packages from the Command Line" **[Hack #58]** for information on how to track down the exact package name you need. Once *configure* has detected all the dependencies it needs, run the *setup.sh* script:

```
greenfly@ubuntu:~tovid-0.25$ sudo ./setup.sh
```

Convert the Video

With tovid installed, now it's time to convert the video. The *tovid* arguments are pretty basic. The only wrinkle is that you need to decide whether to use NTSC or PAL formats and which aspect ratio to use for the video so tovid knows how to properly resize the video. Whether to use NTSC or PAL formats depends on where you live (or, more specifically, what your TV uses). If you live in the United States, use NTSC. If you live in Europe or Japan, use PAL.

tovid supports full-screen (4:3), wide-screen (16:9), and theatrical wide-screen (2.35:1) aspect ratios through the -full, -wide, and -panavision options, respectively. Generally speaking, if you are creating a DVD of a home video or TV show, you will probably use -full (which is what *tovid* uses by default if you don't specify the option). If the video source is from a movie, you will use -wide or -panavision, depending on how wide the video is. If you are unsure, run the *idvid* utility that comes with the tovid suite on the video file to output the width and height of the video, and then divide the width by the height:

```
$ idvid  sample.avi
-----------------------------------
idvid video identification script
Version 0.25
Written in 2004 by Eric Pierce
http://tovid.sourceforge.net/
-----------------------------------
Gathering video information. This may take several minutes,
so please be patient...
=======================================================
File: sample.avi
Width: 512 pixels
Height: 384 pixels
...
$
```

In this example, the video aspect ratio is 512/384, or 4:3.

With the aspect ratio chosen, run *tovid* with the -dvd option to create the new DVD-compatible MPEG2 file. *tovid* also takes as arguments -in

followed by the input file, and -out followed by the name to give the output file (without any file extensions):

```
$ tovid -dvd -ntsc -full -in sample.avi -out output
Probing video for information. This may take several minutes...
Input file is 512 x 384 at 23.976 fps.
Reported running time is 1267 seconds.
Source is not 29.970 fps. Adjusting to 29.970 fps.
Scaling and/or padding with letterbox bars
Scaling 512 x 384 directly to 720 x 480
The encoding process is estimated to require 886 MB of disk space.
You currently have 21396 MB available in this directory.
==========================================================
Testing mplayer stability with -vc dummy option:
Test succeeded!
Creating WAV of audio stream with the following command:
mplayer -quiet -vo null -ao pcm "sample.avi" -vc dummy -ao pcm:file=stream.
wav
==========================================================
==========================================================
Encoding WAV to ac3 format with the following command:
ffmpeg -i stream.wav -ab 224 -ar 48000 -ac 2 -acodec ac3 -y "output.ac3"
Audio encoding finished successfully
==========================================================
Creating and encoding video stream using the following commands:
nice -n 0 mplayer -benchmark -nosound -noframedrop -noautosub -vo yuv4mpeg -
vf-add pp=hb/vb/dr/al:f -vf-add hqdn3d -vf-add scale=720:480 "sample.avi"
cat stream.yuv | yuvfps -r 30000:1001 -n -v 0 | nice -n 0 mpeg2enc -M 2 -a 2
-f 8 -b 8000 -g 4 -G 11 -D 10 -F 4 -v 0 -n n -4 2 -2 1 -q 5 --keep-hf -o
"output.m2v"
```

If you have more than one video you would like to convert, you can use the *tovid-batch* command instead. *tovid-batch* takes the same arguments as *tovid*, except that you use -infiles instead of -in and you don't specify an output filename; *tovid-batch* will determine the output filename based on the input filename. So if you had a directory of full-screen *.avi* files you wanted to convert to DVD, run this:

```
$ tovid-batch -dvd -full -ntsc -infiles *.avi
```

Create the XML File

The next step is to create a proper *.xml* file to describe the DVD structure. You can use the *makexml* tool that is included with tovid to create an XML file that is compatible with the *dvdauthor* tool. *makexml* supports more options when used for DVDs.

Table 3-3 lists the DVD-specific options.

Table 3-3. makexml arguments

Argument	Function
-group *videofile1* *videofile2* ... -endgroup	List of video files to include as one single title. This is useful if you have split a movie into several video files.
-titlesets	Forces the creation of a separate titleset per title. This is useful if the titles of a DVD have different video formats—e.g., PAL + NTSC or 4:3 + 16:9. If used with menus, there must be a -topmenu option that specifies a menu file with an entry for each of the titlesets.
-chapters *n*	Creates a chapter every *n* minutes within the video. This option can be put at any position in a file list and is valid for all subsequent titles until a new -chapters option is encountered. Using this option may increase burn time, since the duration of the video is calculated.

These options are generally for special cases, apart from the last option. By default, *makexml* won't define chapters in your DVD, which means you won't be able to easily skip through it. To add chapters, use the -chapters option and specify an interval, such as 5 or 10 minutes. That way, you can more quickly skip through the DVD. To create an XML file for the sample video with a chapter every five minutes, type:

```
$ makexml -dvd -chapters 5  output.mpg output
---------------------------------------------
makexml
A script to generate XML for authoring a VCD, SVCD, or DVD.
Part of the tovid suite, version 0.18b
Written in 2004 by Eric Pierce
http://tovid.sourceforge.net/
---------------------------------------------
Adding title: output.mpg as title number 1 of titleset 1
Calculating the duration of the video using the following command:
idvid -terse "output.mpg"
This may take a few minutes, so please be patient...
The duration of the video is 00:21:07
Closing titleset 1 with 1 title(s).
=============================================
Done. The resulting XML was written to output.xml.
You can create the DVD filesystem by running the command:
    dvdauthor -x output.xml
    Thanks for using makexml!
```

where output.mpg is the name of the movie to work on and output is the name of the XML file to create (the *.xml* is appended automatically).

Create the DVD Filesystem Structure

With the XML file created, the next step is to use *dvdauthor* to create the DVD filesystem. *dvdauthor* has a number of options you can use to create

special DVD filesystems, but since *makexml* has already done the work for you, you can just pass your XML file to *dvdauthor* as an argument. *makexml* also listed the appropriate command to use near the end of its output, so to create a DVD filesystem for this example, type:

```
$ dvdauthor -x output.xml
DVDAuthor::dvdauthor, version 0.6.11.
Build options: gnugetopt magick iconv freetype fribidi
Send bugs to

INFO: Locale=en_US
INFO: Converting filenames to ISO-8859-1
INFO: dvdauthor creating VTS
STAT: Picking VTS 01

STAT: Processing output.mpg...
STAT: VOBU 3184 at 529MB, 1 PGCS
INFO: Video pts = 0.178 .. 1268.077
INFO: Audio[0] pts = 0.178 .. 1267.506
STAT: VOBU 3194 at 530MB, 1 PGCS
INFO: Generating VTS with the following video attributes:
INFO: MPEG version: mpeg2
INFO: TV standard: ntsc
INFO: Aspect ratio: 4:3
INFO: Resolution: 720x480
INFO: Audio ch 0 format: ac3/2ch, 48khz drc

STAT: fixed 3194 VOBUS
INFO: dvdauthor creating table of contents
INFO: Scanning output/VIDEO_TS/VTS_01_0.IFO
```

dvdauthor will create a directory named *output* and store the *AUDIO_TS* and *VIDEO_TS* DVD filesystem there. If you want to test the DVD before you burn it, you can use *mplayer* to play from this filesystem with the -dvd-device option:

```
$ mplayer dvd://1 -dvd-device output/
```

This command plays the first title from the DVD filesystem under the output directory. If you want to play a different title, specify it on the command line.

Burn the DVD

Now it's time to burn the file structure to DVD. With K3b **[Hack #34]**, click File → New Project → New Video DVD Project. Find your DVD filesystem in the top pane and then drag and drop the files inside the *AUDIO_TS* (if any) and *VIDEO_TS* directories into their respective directories in the bottom pane. Then click the Burn button to set the DVD-burning options and, finally, to burn the filesystem to DVD.

If you want to burn the DVD from the command line, you need to install *dvdrtools*, which is a fork of the *cdrecord* utility that is designed to support recordable DVD drives. *dvdrtools* is already packaged for Ubuntu, so install it with your preferred package manager.

Once *dvdrtools* is installed, the first step is to use the included *mkisofs* utility to create a DVD image out of your file structure:

```
$ mkisofs -dvd-video -udf -o dvd.iso output/
```

With the *dvd.iso* file created, you can locate the *dvd.iso* file in your file browser, right-click it, and select "Burn to DVD." Otherwise, if you prefer the command line, use the *dvdrecord* utility to burn it:

```
$ dvdrecord -dao speed=2 dev=/dev/dvdrw dvd.iso
```

Replace the *dev=/dev/dvdrw* option with the correct values for your DVD burner.

With the DVD created, pop it in your DVD player and test your results.

HACK #37 Connect to a Digital Camera

Under Ubuntu, connecting to your digital camera is just about as easy as plugging it in.

We've used digital cameras under Linux in the past, and while it hasn't been too difficult to get pictures off of them, when we wanted to automate the process, we had to do a considerable amount of hacking. Not so under Ubuntu, where importing images from a camera, whether it's a USB storage device or not, is just a matter of plugging it in and clicking a few buttons. In this hack, we'll describe the general process to connect to a digital camera under Ubuntu.

Before we go into the individual steps in the process, we should mention that not all digital cameras are created equal. You can categorize digital cameras under Linux into two categories: cameras that have USB-storage-device support and cameras that don't. Cameras that have USB-storage-device support appear as standard USB hard drives when you plug them into a computer. For instance, if you plug such a device into a Windows or Mac machine, you can browse through the camera just as if it were a USB thumb drive. Under Ubuntu, this isn't too different; these devices will show up as a hard drive, and you can browse through them as such. There are also a number of cameras that don't tout USB storage device support. For these cameras, you will have to rely on Ubuntu's *libgphoto* libraries to communicate with the cameras over their specific protocols.

For the most part, under Ubuntu, we've had pretty good success importing photos, even on relatively new digital cameras that required *libgphoto*, but the best way to find out about your particular camera's support is simply to plug it in.

To import photos from your digital camera on Ubuntu, just plug in the USB connector and power on the camera. If Ubuntu recognizes the device, it will present you with a dialog similar to the one in Figure 3-9. If you have already imported your photos, then you can click Ignore; otherwise, click Import Photos. The window that appears next will vary depending on which type of camera you have. These are different enough that we'll go into each of them.

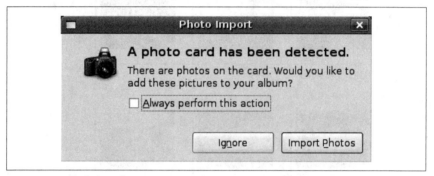

Figure 3-9. The dialog Ubuntu presents when you plug in a digital camera

Import from a Non-USB-Storage-Device Camera

If your camera does not have USB-storage-device support, Ubuntu will need to perform an intermediary step to import the photos from your drive. After you select Import Photos, Ubuntu will present you with a window like the one in Figure 3-10. This program uses *libgphoto* to pull the photos off of the camera. (While this program will allow you to rotate photos, we recommend you wait until the next step and rotate them in the gThumb program.) Select where you would like to import these photos from the Destination drop-down menu and click Import. Ubuntu will then import each photo from the camera into a new directory in the destination that is conveniently timestamped so that you can keep track of when the photos were imported.

Once Ubuntu finishes importing the photos, it will open the gThumb program with that directory selected. Figure 3-11 shows how gThumb presents your photos in thumbnail format. From here, you click the Rotate button (or click Tools → Rotate), display a slideshow of every photo, or

Figure 3-10. Import photos using libgphoto from this window

double-click on a particular photo to take a closer look. Since the import program already copied all of the photos off of your camera, you can now disconnect it whenever you please.

Import from a USB-Storage-Device Camera

If your camera has USB-storage-device support, Ubuntu will bypass the intermediary step of importing the photos and instead take you directly to a gThumb display of your image directory, as shown in Figure 3-11. From here, you can rotate images, view slideshows, and examine your images; however, note that any changes you make are made on the camera itself. If

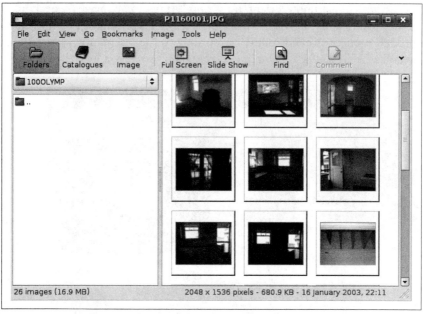

Figure 3-11. gThumb displaying the imported photos

you want to copy the files to your computer, you will need to create a directory to store the photos; then you can drag and drop the photos from gThumb into your new directory.

> Before you disconnect a camera that has USB storage device support, be sure to click Places → Computer, locate the camera's drive in the window, then right-click on it and select Eject to be sure that any files have been synced and that the camera is safe to unplug.

Automatically Rotate Your Photos with gThumb

One nice feature of some newer digital cameras is the ability to store the orientation of the camera when a picture is taken. The image will then have stored within its metadata information that says not only when the picture was taken, but whether you took the picture in portrait or landscape mode. If your camera supports this feature, you can save a lot of effort rotating images within gThumb. Type Ctrl-A to select all of the images in the directory, then click Tools → Rotate to open the Rotate Images dialog. Then

check the "Adjust photo orientation" and "Apply to all images" checkboxes in that window, as shown in Figure 3-12. Click Apply, and gThumb will go through each photo and rotate it according to the orientation stored in the metadata. This can be quite a time-saver when you have a lot of images.

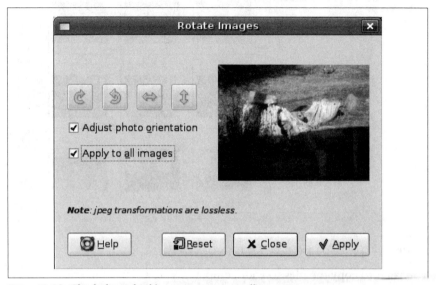

Figure 3-12. Check these checkboxes to automatically rotate images

## CHAPTER FOUR

Mobile Ubuntu

Hacks 38–46

Ubuntu is a mobile-friendly Linux distribution. It will detect and configure almost any wireless hardware you can throw at it. In some cases, you will run into some hardware that, because its maker won't provide open source developers the information they need, can't run on Ubuntu. However, you can usually fiddle with the proprietary Windows drivers to get it working. And once you do get your wireless adapter up and running, you'll need to configure it to work with the various Wi-Fi networks you use. The hacks in this chapter cover all these topics and more.

For anyone who spends a lot of time away from a power source, power management is a major concern. This chapter also shows you how to put your computer into sleep and deep sleep, and provides some tricks on prolonging your battery life while you are away from a power source. You'll also learn how to work with notebook-specific peripherals, such as PC Cards and hotswappable optical drives.

HACK #38 Put Your Laptop to Sleep

Close the lid and save some power.

Part of proper power management is the ability to put your laptop to sleep. *ACPI sleep* is defined as a state where the system is still technically powered on, but the screen and hard disk are powered down and the computer is using just enough power to keep the contents of RAM alive. The Ubuntu development team has devoted an immense amount of effort toward getting ACPI power management working properly. As it stands, Ubuntu is power-management-friendly right out of the box, thanks to the recent addition of the *gnome-power-manager* package. It turns out there's not much required to get most modern laptops to sleep and wake up correctly.

Getting Some Sleep

The Dapper Drake release of Ubuntu Linux includes the new *gnome-power-manager* package, which enables ACPI sleep much like the system-tray power applet in Windows. Finally, sleep "just works" in Linux. The *gnome-power-manager* applet is configured to start automatically, and it lives in GNOME's panel notification area. If you right-click on the little battery icon, you'll see a menu pop up, as shown in Figure 4-1.

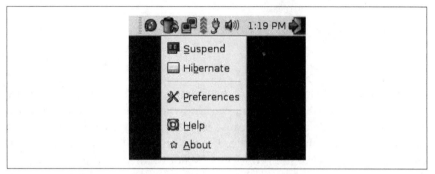

Figure 4-1. gnome-power-manager in action

This deceptively simple little application gives you a lot of control over your laptop's sleep behavior. If you click on Preferences, you'll see the Power Management Preferences dialog box shown in Figure 4-2. In this dialog's Sleep tab, you can configure different behavior depending on whether you're plugged into AC power or running on battery. One of the most interesting features is your ability to control the backlight brightness of your laptop's screen depending on the machine's power state. It happens to work out that a large consumer of power in a laptop is the screen's backlight, so being able to automatically turn down that lamp while on battery will help squeeze more runtime out of the system while it's unplugged.

The Options tab (see Figure 4-3) is where you can set the default type of sleep you wish for the system to use, as well as what actions will engage the sleep mechanism. For this hack, the default sleep type is set to Suspend, which refers to ACPI sleep. (Hibernate **[Hack #39]** is a totally different type of sleep mechanism.) If you wish, under the Actions section of the dialog box, you can set the system to automatically sleep when the laptop lid is closed. This is a very handy feature if you're on the go: simply shut the lid and run off to your next appointment; then open the lid later, and the machine will wake up without any intervention.

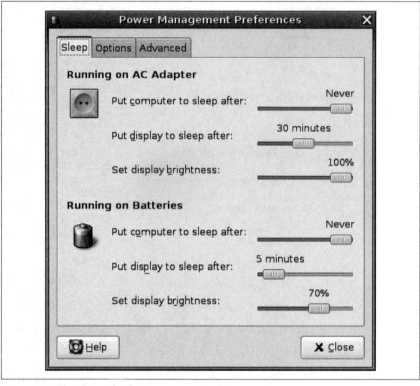

Figure 4-2. The Sleep tab of gnome-power-manager

The Advanced tab of the dialog (Figure 4-4) controls the notification icon's behavior. If you want the icon to appear only when you're charging or discharging, or you want to turn off the icon altogether, here's where you change those settings.

 If you're not seeing the notification icon, perhaps it's because you're plugged into AC power. If you'd like to see the applet all the time, unplug your laptop for a moment and the icon should appear. You can then use the Advanced tab to change the notification icon settings.

When you have all your settings configured to your liking, simply click the Close button, and the dialog box will close, saving your configuration changes.

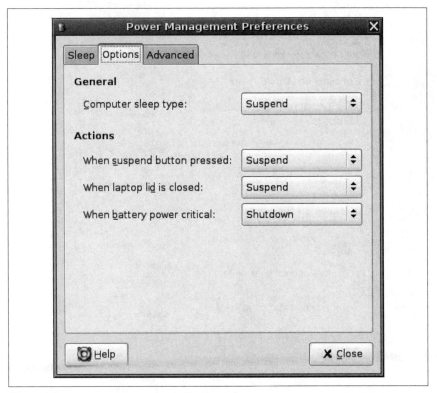

Figure 4-3. gnome-power-manager's Options tab

Testing ACPI Sleep

Your system is now ready for you to test sleep mode. Ensure that your system is running on battery; then simply shut the lid of the laptop and see what happens. You should hear the hard disk power down, and one of the power LEDs should indicate a power-state change by blinking or some other method. Hopefully, your machine went to sleep properly. Now you need to see if it wakes up correctly. Simply open the lid, and the computer should start waking up. When it's ready for use, you'll be prompted for your system password by *gnome-screensaver*. Enter your password, and your system should be in the exact same state as it was when you powered it off.

Thanks to the hard work of the Ubuntu developers, something that used to be extremely difficult to accomplish in Linux has been made very easy.

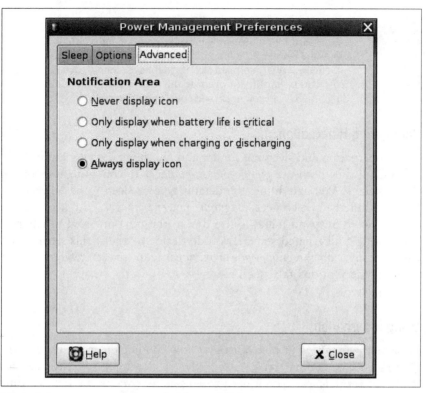

Figure 4-4. gnome-power-manager's Advanced dialog

 ### HACK #39 Hibernate Your Laptop

Sleeping is a good way to pause, but it still uses power. Hibernate mode lets you save the contents of memory to disk so you can resume later on.

In "Put Your Laptop to Sleep" **[Hack #38]**, you learned how Ubuntu supports ACPI sleep. However, because ACPI sleep does require a trickle of power to keep the CPU and RAM alive, it may not be desirable in all situations. Hibernate has been designed as the complement to ACPI sleep. It takes the contents of RAM and saves them to the system's swap partition. As a result, it requires absolutely zero power to maintain that hibernated state. There is a downside to hibernating a machine, however. Due to the fact that the system saves the contents of RAM before powering off, and then loads the contents of RAM after the kernel loads on reboot, it does take a fair amount of time to enter and exit the hibernated state. However, hibernating is still faster than powering off and restarting your machine, and there's the added benefit of saving application state.

Since hibernation saves the exact contents of RAM to your swap partition, the size of your swap partition *must be larger* than the amount of RAM you have in the machine. Ubuntu configures this automatically if you have done a default installation, but if you override the default partitioner during installation, you need to keep this point in mind.

Configuring Hibernation

Since hibernation and sleep are similar and use the underlying Linux ACPI subsystem, they both use *gnome-power-manager* to configure and control their settings. You can adjust the default type of sleep to be hibernation from within the preferences of *gnome-power-manager*, but keeping the default set to Suspend makes sense due to the time involved in entering and exiting a hibernated state. If you do decide to adjust this setting, you can right-click on the *gnome-power-manager* icon, select Preferences, and click on the Options tab (see Figure 4-3 in "Put Your Laptop to Sleep" [Hack #38]).

Using Hibernation

Now that you have your preferences set how you like them, it's time to test hibernation. Assuming you're using the stock Ubuntu preferences for *gnome-power-manager*, you'll need to engage hibernation by right-clicking on the *gnome-power-manager* applet and selecting Hibernate. Once you do, the system will immediately dim the screen, and you should hear a good deal of hard-disk activity. Once the disk stops churning, the system will power off. At this point, the system is in hibernate mode and can be left in this state indefinitely without using any battery power. To exit the hibernated state, simply power on the system normally. The bootloader will come up, and the kernel will boot normally, until it detects a RAM image on the swap partition. At that point, the system will load up the RAM image and should return to where you left it. Typical times to enter hibernation run between 30 seconds and 1 minute, and times to exit hibernation (including the BIOS test) run about the same.

Between sleep and hibernation, you have all the great power management capabilities at your disposal.

If your system is configured to boot multiple operating systems, you need to be careful here. In theory, you should be able to hibernate your Ubuntu system and then boot into a different operating system. But this is fundamentally risky: if you change anything on the Ubuntu partition, you'll be in heaps of trouble. And if you're sharing a swap partition between Ubuntu and another Linux distribution, you'll be in a world of trouble if that other Linux distribution boots up, since it will erase your hibernated state (or may itself try to resume from that hibernated state). Play it safe: if you are hibernated, don't boot into anything except the system you hibernated from.

Prolong Your Battery Life
HACK #40
Throttle your CPU, dim your display, and slow your hard drive to conserve precious battery power.

GNOME has a built-in CPU-frequency-monitor applet that will show you the current speed of your processor. This is great for laptops that have CPUs that can support dynamic frequency scaling. Additionally, the same applet will also let you alter the processor-speed governors and/or lock in the speed at a fixed frequency. This will let you override the built-in processor-speed governors for maximum performance or maximum battery life, depending on your needs at the time. This isn't overclocking or anything that's possibly damaging to your CPU; rather, this will let you use the built-in SpeedStep or other CPU-throttling techniques to their maximum.

This hack does not work for Transmeta-equipped CPUs with LongRun technology. However, Ubuntu does have *longrun* and other tools available via *apt-get* for these processors.

To be able to switch CPU speeds, you must set the *cpufreq-selector* program to be *suid root*:

```
bill@defiant:~$ sudo chmod +s /usr/bin/cpufreq-selector
```

This may be a slight security issue. If there is a vulnerability in *cpufreq-selector*, anyone who exploits it has the potential to get *root* access on the machine. See "Manage Security Updates" [Hack #68] for information on keeping up-to-date with the latest security fixes.

Once you've done this, enable the CPU Frequency Monitor if you don't have it running already. Right-click on your top GNOME panel and select "Add to Panel." Then select the CPU Frequency Monitor applet from the list and click on Add. The applet will appear in your panel. At this point, you can left-click on the applet and adjust the current CPU speed governor. If you right-click on the applet and select Preferences, you can change the menu that's displayed from Governors to "Frequencies and Governors." After setting this, you'll be able to tailor your CPU speed for any situation you may encounter (see Figure 4-5).

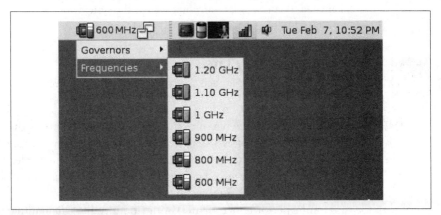

Figure 4-5. The CPU Frequency Monitor in action

Your choice of Governor puts some constraints on your CPU speed choices. If you want to be able to specify the CPU speed yourself, choose the *user-space* governor, and then select the desired speed from the Frequencies menu. The *ondemand* and *conservative* governors adjust the speed based on demand, but *conservative* won't raise the CPU speed as quickly as *onde-mand*. The *performance* and *powersave* governors will keep the CPU speed at either the maximum or minimum.

HACK #41 Get Proprietary Wireless Cards Working

If your computer has a Wi-Fi card that's not Linux-friendly, don't fret. Ndiswrapper and ndisgtk will let you use that card under Ubuntu by encapsulating the native Windows driver.

In "Roam Wirelessly" [Hack #42], you'll see that Ubuntu ships with built-in drivers for a good deal of the wireless network cards on the market today, such as the Intel "ipw" line of miniPCI adapters and the Prism 2/3–based PCMCIA network adapters. If you happen to use a computer that's equipped with such hardware, Ubuntu's wireless networking will likely "just